# The Land and People of
# BOLIVIA

BOLIVIA, part of the fabled empire of the Incas, was conquered by the Spaniards in the sixteenth century for its precious metals and ruled by Spain for three hundred years. The mixture of European and indigenous Indian cultures has left its mark on many aspects of Bolivian life, including the ethnic makeup of the people.

The Bolivians—most of whom are at least part Indian—live mainly in the arid Andean foothills, two miles or more above sea level, preferring the homeland of their ancestors to the fertile but unfamiliar Bolivian lowlands.

Political instability has plagued Bolivia since independence from Spain, and the yield from the mines is decreasing. Nonetheless, Bolivia is moving into the twentieth century, developing unexploited natural resources and bringing new benefits to its people, though life in city and village retains much of the flavor of the past.

This book introduces the colorful traditions and customs of the people; the spectacular diversity of the land; and the turbulent history that made this fifth largest South American country the fascinating place it is today.

# PORTRAITS OF THE NATIONS SERIES

# The Land and People of
# BOLIVIA

by Leslie F. Warren

PORTRAITS OF THE NATIONS SERIES

J. B. LIPPINCOTT COMPANY
Philadelphia          New York

For the use of photographs on the following pages, the author gratefully credits: L. Archer, 94, 96; OAS, 41, 91, 143; José Pierola, 13, 26, 76, 84, 114, 118, 135; Ultima Hora, 48, 51, 54, 58, 73, 80, 109; United Nations, 15, 19, 23, 28, 39, 70, 86, 88, 105, 123, 130; USAID, Bolivia, 34, 62, 148, 150.

*c1*
*918.4*
*WAR*
*12.78*

U.S. Library of Congress Cataloging in Publication Data

Warren, Leslie F
  The land and people of Bolivia.

  (Portraits of the nations series)
  SUMMARY: An introduction to the geography, history, resources, people, and major cities of South America's fifth largest country.
  1. Bolivia—Juvenile literature. [1. Bolivia] I. Title.
F3308.5.W37     918.4'03'5     74-8911
ISBN-0-397-31578-3

To Clarisse
who made the journey with me

# Contents

# The Land and People of
# BOLIVIA

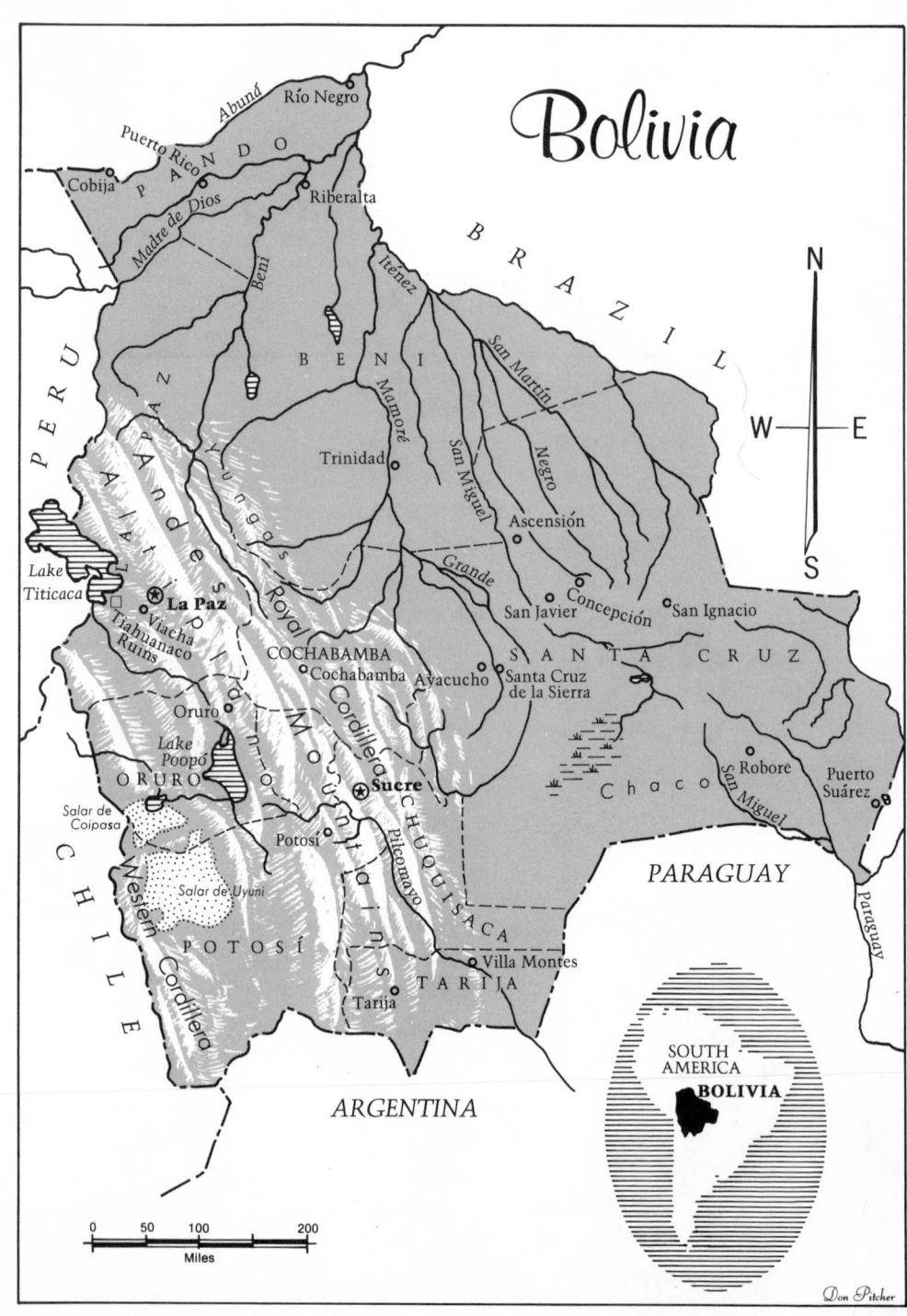

# 1

# High in the Andes

Bolivia is South America's fifth largest country, as big as the two largest "united" states, Texas and California, put together. It has grassy flatlands where thousands of cattle roam virtually untended, humid jungles cut by great twisting rivers, upland valleys where the climate is springlike all year around. But the most important part of the country by far lies high in the Andes. There, in the chill, desolate tableland called the *altiplano,* and on the slopes of the massive Andean mountain chains, or *cordilleras,* ranging on either side, live two-thirds of Bolivia's five million people. The country's history, its government, its industry and commerce, all are centered there, two miles or more above the level of the sea.

Stretching some four thousand miles from Colombia to the southern tip of Chile, the Andes are one of the longest and highest mountain chains in the world. In Peru they split into two ranges that run through Bolivia to join again farther south where they form the boundary between Chile and Argentina. The Eastern Cordillera, known also as the Cordillera Real, or Royal Cordillera, averages 18,000 feet in height. On a glacier below one peak, 17,700-foot-high Chacaltaya, is the world's highest ski run, starting at 16,000 feet.

There are other giants, towering so high they are perpetually mantled with snow even though they rise in the midst of the Tropics. Among them are Huayna Potosí; Murarata, called "the headless one" because of its curious flat top; majestic Illampu, soaring 21,275 feet; and Illimani, 21,180 feet high, standing guard over the city of La Paz. Out of the Cordillera Occidental, or Western Cordillera, which Bolivia shares with its neighbor Chile, rises the volcano of Sajama, Bolivia's highest peak, thrusting up 21,500 feet.

At such lofty heights, the leap of the elusive *vicuña,* the now rare relative of the larger *llama,* and the gliding shadow of the condor, with the largest wingspread of any bird in the world, are the only movements likely to catch the eye.

Far below, at an altitude of a mere twelve thousand feet, is the altiplano, or high plain, stretching five hundred miles from north to south and eighty to one hundred miles between the two cordilleras. Ancient peoples created a great civilization there, of which only traces remain. Where these people came from and what happened to them nobody knows. Later, the Incas extended their realm throughout the altiplano and the surrounding highlands. The Spanish *conquistadores,* conquerors, in their turn also came to dominate the area.

To be sure, Bolivia is not all mountains. The low-lying eastern region called the Oriente covers three-fifths of the country. Most of it is semiarid plains and swampy savannas, and the northern part is tropical forest, with coiling rivers interrupted by swift rapids or sluggish stretches that trap treacherous floating trees, making transportation difficult. The Oriente has fertile farmlands and underground resources such as gas and oil and iron that may one day make it Bolivia's richest and most important area. In fact, it is already on its

The alpaca, like the vicuña and llama, belongs to the camel family and is native to Bolivia.

way to becoming just that, and better roads to connect it with the rest of the country could speed the process.

Between the Oriente and the highlands is an intermediate zone of broad open *valles* in the south, and narrow, almost vertical gorges called *yungas* to the north. In the high valleys, at altitudes of eight to nine thousand feet, the climate is always temperate, so agriculture thrives. Also, the passes over the

Eastern Cordillera are relatively easy. The yungas, on the other hand, rise almost straight up out of tropic vegetation and are frequently shrouded in mist. What few roads exist are unpaved and cling to the steep rock walls with many sharp twists and turns. Travel in this section of Bolivia is extremely precarious. Trucks and other vehicles meeting on the roads sometimes have to back up and then pass each other with the utmost caution, or they may slip over the edge to plunge thousands of feet below.

Bolivia's divided landscape is thus full of contrasts. But of its three principal geographical regions, it is the Andean highlands that are most important today and that give it such striking characteristics. The heights alone are enough to awe visitors. Of Bolivia's seven most important cities, all but one are higher than Mexico City, the highest big city in North America. The fabled city of Potosí is a thousand feet higher than Lhasa, capital of Tibet in Asia's Himalaya Mountains. And Bolivia's capitals—it has two—could both look down on mile-high Denver. The official capital of Sucre is 9,400 feet high; and La Paz, the country's largest city, where the executive and legislative branches of government are located, at an altitude of 12,140 feet is the highest true capital anywhere in the world. So "thin" is the air in La Paz that newcomers to the city often have difficulty getting enough oxygen and have to breathe it from bottles until their lungs adjust to its scarcity in the atmosphere.

The world's highest stretch of railroad is in Bolivia, running through a pass 15,809 feet high over the Western Cordillera. Also lying in Bolivia is half of the world's highest navigable body of water—Lake Titicaca. Few trees will grow at its altitude of 12,664 feet, so fishermen use reeds found at the lake's edges instead of wood to make their boats.

Lake Titicaca and the surrounding altiplano form one of the strangest bits of landscape anywhere on the globe. It is stark, foreboding, full of mysteries. For example, only a dozen miles from the lake are the oldest architectural ruins in the Americas, all that is left of a massive complex of structures called Tiahuanaco. Where its builders came from and when, how they acquired the skills needed to erect their monumental buildings, and what finally happened to them are questions that have never been answered. Stories are told that Inca treasures were dumped into the lake to save them from the clutches of the Spanish conquistadores. But no treasure has been found. Nor has any acceptable explanation been offered for what is happening to Lake Titicaca itself. It is shrinking, although the amount of water entering it from surrounding snowcapped mountains appears to be greater than the quantity lost through drainage and evaporation.

Indian women of the altiplano wash clothes in a mountain stream.

At the southern end of the lake is the town of Guaqui, Bolivia's principal port. Bolivia has no seacoast, as a glance at a map will show. (It had one once, but lost it in a war with Chile.) On the map also, the general shape of Bolivia will be seen as a rough triangle, with a piece bitten off at the bottom right-hand angle. This "missing bite" was also once Bolivian. It is the Gran Chaco territory, which Bolivia lost in a war with Paraguay. Actually, Bolivia at one time was almost twice its present size. Besides the areas lost in wars, it ceded territory to Brazil and Argentina. For example, Bolivia gave up the area called Acre in exchange for Brazil's agreement to build a railroad around the falls of the Madeira River so that Bolivian jungle rubber could be shipped to world markets via the Amazon.

Brazil's present-day territory of Acre lies northwest of Bolivia and is separated from it by the Abuna River and certain of its tributaries. Rivers also form most of the boundary between Bolivia and Brazilian territory on its northeast flank. These rivers are the Mamoré and Guaporé, affluents of the Madeira, which flows into the Atlantic through the Amazon system, and the Río Grande and the Pilcomayo, which flow southeast into the Paraguay and Plate River system. The countries of Paraguay and Argentina bound Bolivia on the south, and Chile and Peru border the country on the west.

Nearly all of Bolivia's hundreds of rivers rise in the Cordillera Real, which is a relatively short distance from the Pacific Ocean. But their waters empty into the Atlantic after flowing more than a thousand miles east. For a rough idea of what Bolivia is like, try to imagine the United States with its principal cities and most of its people crowded into the Rocky Mountains area and a few small settlements scattered to the east. To complete the picture, think of the Mississippi and virtually every other important river flowing from the Rockies clear across the continent, through territory belonging to other nations, to discharge into the Atlantic!

The highland area where most of Bolivia's peoples live is truly an inhospitable one. In fact, so bleak is the landscape and so sparse the vegetation of the altiplano that nothing man or his animals could use might seem to come from there. Yet one of the world's most important food crops, the potato, originated there. (Some scientists believe that corn was first developed in Bolivia also.) Nonetheless, centuries ago, somehow a mode of life was worked out that permitted people to exist in that harsh environment. Potatoes—Bolivia has over one hundred varieties—and native grains provided food staples, and llamas and *alpacas,* which together with the smaller vicuñas and *guanacos* are the only members of the camel family native to the Americas, were domesticated. They provided—and still provide—wool and leather for clothing, meat and milk for cheese, and they are a means of transportation besides. In the wood-short altiplano, their dung serves as a smokeless fuel. Another small animal which at one time or other you may have kept as a pet—the cavy or guinea pig—is also a native of Bolivia, and it is another source of food.

With such meager resources, men learned to survive on the altiplano on a scale not much lower than that of many of its inhabitants today. Nonetheless, there is great wealth in Bolivia's highlands, but it is mostly underground, within the mountains themselves. It was the lust for mineral wealth, chiefly gold and silver, that lured the conquistadores to the Andes, bringing in their wake the destruction of the vast empire ruled by the Incas that stretched from Ecuador south through Peru and Bolivia all the way into Chile and Argentina. At first, the Spanish were content simply to cart off all the gold and silver objects they could lay their hands on. When these ran out, they forced the native peoples to work the mines as virtual slaves.

Today gold is scarce, and silver is mined chiefly as a by-product of tin. Antimony, lead, bismuth, tungsten, and copper are among the other minerals that Bolivia supplies to the industrial world. Although mining has steadily become less profitable, it is still Bolivia's most important industry, providing jobs for half a million people. However, another mineral, which could bring the country more riches than all the silver and tin, may lie deep under the altiplano. Oil engineers are exploring for petroleum, already produced in eastern Bolivia, and one test well has been sunk more than twelve thousand feet. At that depth, however, it still only reaches to the level of the sea!

As varied as is Bolivia's landscape, so are its people in their ethnic background and ways of living. A few are pure descendants of the Spaniards, and there is a sprinkling of other Europeans, especially Germans, as well as Japanese colonists in the Oriente. One quarter to a third of the Bolivians have sprung from marriages between the Spanish and the native Aymara and Quechua peoples. Called *cholos,* they are among Bolivia's most enterprising and dynamic inhabitants. An example is the tin baron, the late Simón Patiño, who started his career as a simple miner and became one of the richest men in the world before the government took over his mines.

However, a majority of the Bolivians—perhaps as many as 65 percent—are Aymara and Quechua *indios,* Indians, who cling stubbornly to the ways of their ancestors, many speaking no other language but their own. Their music, their art, and many of their customs, such as the use by men of tight-fitting woollen caps with big flaps to cover their ears, date back to the days of the Incas and even before. Some of their more recent ancestors, however, adopted certain Western styles of clothing, still preserved in Bolivia centuries after they went out of style elsewhere. The Indian women in their bright-colored voluminous skirts and shawls sport old-fashioned headgear of which they are extremely proud. Hats of the Aymara women look like derbies, in brown or black, and those of the Quechuas resemble the wide-brimmed "stovepipe" types of Abraham Lincoln's time, except that they are white instead of

A Quechua woman and an Aymara woman sort pieces of ore at the San Jose tin mine.

black. In Sucre, you will find Indian men wearing hats that are copies in felt of the metal helmets used by the conquistadores.

Today Bolivians refer to their Indian population as *campesinos,* small farmers, and indeed farming is how most of them manage to scratch out a living. On tiny plots, often clinging to hillsides so steep no tractor could ever drive up them, they raise potatoes, barley, and the native grains of *quinoa* and *canahui,* reputedly highly nutritive. In the valles where the land is not too high or the climate too cold, they grow corn and other vegetables, peanuts, and fruits such as peaches, avocados, figs, and olives. In the yungas pineapples, papayas, bananas, and citrus fruits grow everywhere. What produce the campesinos do not consume themselves they bring to town to sell at *ferias,* or open-air markets, along with flowers and beautiful sweaters, capes, and shawls made by the women from llama or alpaca wool.

The government has been encouraging campesinos to move from the bleak altiplano to the fertile Oriente, where such crops as cotton, tobacco, rice, sugar, and coffee can be produced. Many are doing so, although often reluctantly. However, if the resettlement program succeeds—and it has all appearances of doing so—the Oriente may soon surpass Bolivia's highlands in wealth and importance.

# 2

## La Paz — City in a Canyon

La Paz is Bolivia's largest city, its commercial and financial hub, and the principal center of government. (Although Sucre is the official capital, of the three branches of government only the judiciary functions there.) Before the days of air travel, La Paz was one of the hardest cities in the world to reach. One approach was from the east, by river from Buenos Aires in Argentina up the Rio de la Plata, then the Paraná, and finally the Paraguay. But that still left miles and miles of swampy plains and savannas to cross before climbing through the high valleys over the Eastern Cordillera and down to the stark altiplano. Early Spanish and Portuguese adventurers and missionaries came this difficult and tiresome way, and government officials followed this route when what is now Bolivian territory was part of Spain's Viceroyalty of La Plata.

Today a railroad stretches across Brazil to the Bolivian city of Santa Cruz de la Sierra, and another from Argentina reaches all the way to La Paz. Overland travel from the east is thus easier, although part of the journey must be made either on unpaved roads or rail lines subject to landslides.

Another land approach to La Paz is from the west, and this is the most interesting way to get there. You can choose from several routes, each of which takes you through some of the world's most spectacular scenery. You board a train on Chile's arid northern Pacific seacoast, at either Antofagasta or farther north at Arica. You can also enter Bolivia via Peru, traveling by train from Mollendo on the coast to Puno, Peru's port on Lake Titicaca. From there you cross the lake overnight by steamer. When you wake up, you are in Bolivia, at the shabby little port of Guaqui, a two-hour train ride across the altiplano from La Paz.

Fascinating as it may be, however, traveling to La Paz by land takes several days and may not leave you time for everything there is to see and do in the strange world of Bolivia. In that case, you will want to fly. If you leave from New York, you will head south and just a bit east. (It may surprise you to learn that practically all of South America, including its Pacific coastline, lies east of Washington, D.C.!) Be sure to take along warm clothing. Though you will be going to the Tropics, the nights are cold on the altiplano, even in summer. Dark glasses are also useful. The brilliance of the sun reflected from the snow at the great heights you will be visiting can blur your vision.

The long flight from the United States takes most of the day, and there are brief stops at cities such as Quito in Ecuador, Bogotá in Colombia, or Lima in Peru. Finally, after hours of flying over and sometimes between towering Andean peaks, your plane approaches La Paz. It lands at the modern El Alto Aeropuerto, at 13,300 feet the highest commercial airport in the world. How drab and flat the landscape seems! Yet only a mile or so away the land plunges abruptly 1,000 feet down to La Paz. In fact, the city seems to have been built inside a crater. Actually, the depression is a gorge or canyon, carved by millions of years of erosion by the Choqueyapu River as it cut through the crumbly altiplano soil, which was laid down so recently in geological time that it was never compressed into rock.

The view from the rim of the altiplano is stupendous. On a clear day—rare in the rainy summer months from November to April—you can look directly across to a cordillera, a great barrier of peaks standing guard over the city below: Illampu, Chacaltaya, and Illimani. Almost directly under your feet is La Paz. Tin-roofed houses painted blue, pink, yellow, or green cling to the bare gray slopes of the canyon. Down at the very bottom is a forest of tall buildings in the center of town, giving one the impression that the city sank into the earth under their weight.

View of La Paz from El Alto airport, with Mt. Illimani in the background.

An electric rail line winds down into the city, alongside the only paved highway into and out of La Paz. When important visitors like heads of foreign states use the road, it is closed to all other traffic. And for twenty-four hours before their arrival, painters work furiously whitewashing walls and light poles to make everything along the route seem spic and span.

As you start down the highway by bus or taxi, you wonder how on earth La Paz came to be built in a hole. The reason is that the canyon offers shelter from the chill winds that sweep the altiplano. Thus, in the seventeenth and eighteenth centuries the locale afforded an excellent resting place for the weary packtrains of mules and llamas that transported silver from the mines of Potosí all the way to Cuzco and then Lima, from whence it went to Spain in fleets under convoy. The site was used for this purpose for several years before the village that grew up there was officially declared a city. On October 20, 1548, a Spanish conquistador, Captain Alonso de Mendoza, baptized it with its full name, Nuestra Señora de la Paz, or Our Lady of Peace.

For many years, La Paz was outranked in importance by other Bolivian cities such as Sucre and the mining center of Potosí. Gradually, however, La Paz grew into an important commercial hub. Waterpower supplied by the river attracted industries. Government offices were transferred little by little from Sucre, leaving only the Supreme Court in the old capital. And finally the construction of the railroads from the Pacific coast made La Paz a much more logical entryway into the country than such cities as Sucre and Cochabamba, on the other side of the Andes. These cities may possess greater charm and a more amenable climate than La Paz, but for bustle and excitement they cannot match the city built in the canyon.

Its location in the gorge has brought another advantage to La Paz. Protected from the winds, trees will grow there, although not to any great height except for the eucalyptus and casuarina pines, both imported from Australia early in the present century. You pass through groves of them as you spiral down toward the heart of the city, and you notice how they help soften the otherwise harsh and barren landscape.

Now the road passes offshoots, little man-made plateaus where the poorer residents of the city constructed their colorfully painted brick and adobe homes. You descend farther, past textile mills and other factories. Finally the road broadens into a wide thoroughfare, Avenida Mariscal Santa Cruz, and you are in downtown La Paz. It is a mixture of old and modern, with baroque palaces from the eighteenth century standing shoulder to shoulder with fifteen-story glass and concrete office buildings. Automobiles and other vehicles choke the street, although there are not so many of the former as in richer countries. The newer cars are imports, mostly from Japan; Bolivia is too small to support an auto industry of its own. There are little motorcycle-driven vans, and buses called *coletivos*. There are taxis, of course, including a special kind dubbed *trufis*, a name made up of the initial letters of *transportes rutas fijas*, or transportation along fixed routes. In other countries they might be called jitneys. They follow regular routes, stopping on the way to pick up and let out passengers.

A little way past an obelisk, still scarred with bullet holes from one of Bolivia's frequent revolutions, the avenue changes its name to 16 de Julio, sixteenth of July. Down the middle of the final stretch runs a promenade planted with trees and flowers, making it a favorite stroll for *paceños*, as the residents of La Paz are called, on Sundays. Called the Prado, this section slopes from Plaza Venezuela, with its statue of

A view down the Prado in La Paz.

Simón Bolívar, South America's great hero in its fight for independence from Spain, to the statue of Bolivia's own liberator, Marshal Antonio José de Sucre. Here the finer shops and restaurants of La Paz are located, most of its elegant hotels, and, at the very end, the building housing the "skyscraper" University of San Andrés.

You will probably want to start exploring this fascinating city of 750,000, or nearly a fifth of all Bolivians, at once. But first you need to change some of your money into local currency, which the cashier at your hotel will be happy to do for you. Once called the *peso,* Bolivia's currency was later changed to the *sucre.* Now it is the peso once more, officially the *peso boliviano.* It is worth five United States cents, and there are bills in one-, five-, ten-, twenty-, fifty-, and one-hundred-peso denominations, as well as a one-peso coin. Also there are smaller coins worth a varying number of *centavos,* each centavo, of course, representing one hundredth of a peso.

Supplied with Bolivian money, you can now set out to tour the city. But take your time. La Paz has virtually no level streets, and if you try to climb one of the steep cobblestone sidewalks too fast you will soon be puffing as though you had run a race—except that it takes much longer to catch your breath and begin to breathe normally again. Newcomers to the city frequently are rendered uncomfortable by shortness of breath, headaches, dizziness, and heart palpitations, all symptoms of the "mountain sickness" called *soroche.* Usually it passes after a day of rest with only the lightest of meals, but hotels stand ready to rush oxygen bottles to older victims who start gasping, usually as the result of overexertion. Paceños— at least those descended from Indians—never seem to be bothered. You see why when you notice how thick-chested they are. Generations of living at extremely high altitudes have produced a type of person with a large lung capacity to absorb more oxygen.

Now as you step out into the street, no one seems to be dawdling. Girls and boys hurry by, to and from school, the younger children in their uniforms. Older boys dress in sweaters and blue jeans, and the girls wear maxicoats or attractive capes or *ponchos* made from alpaca wool. Besides students, people from other walks of life and all parts of the country bustle along. Paceño businessmen, shoppers, sellers of lottery tickets; miners from Oruro or Potosí, dressed in their best dark suits with scarves tucked around the neck. (On cold days, the men often wear soft felt hats over their wool caps, or

Indian women wearing *awayos* pause to admire a display of imported kitchen utensils.

*lluchos.*) Indian women from the altiplano villages wear their brown bowler hats and bright *pollera* skirts, and *mantas,* or shawls, draped over their shoulders. Many use an *awayo,* an extra wool or cotton cloth that also goes around the shoulder and is tied in front. Worn this way, they make excellent "shopping bags," with the advantage that the wearer's hands are free to carry more articles. Even babies ride on their mother's backs in this fashion. Here is a woman now getting ready to wrap her small daughter, so you can watch how it is done. She lays the awayo out on the ground, and then the baby, carefully bundled in a soft small blanket, on top. Now she grasps the ends of the awayo to draw it into a sort of hammock. With a twist of her arms, she sends the whole affair, baby and all, circling around her head and onto her back. That's all there is to it!

You follow her into the throng moving up the Prado. You may want to stop at one of the smart shops that sell articles woven from llama or the softer alpaca wool. There are sweaters and warm ponchos, and wall hangings with the stylized designs of the precolonial peoples. The llama or alpaca wool (the latter grows thicker and shorter) is never dyed in this part of Bolivia but left in its natural white, black, browns, and grays to be worked into intricate and beautiful patterns. Many of the same goods, cheaper and of poorer quality, can be found in the Indian Market on Calle Sagárnaga, where dried herbs and articles with "magical" properties, such as preserved llama fetuses, are sold.

Along the sidewalk you pass stands or kiosks selling everything from magazines to razor blades and even food. A favorite snack in La Paz is *anticuchos,* or pieces of beef heart barbecued on a skewer. If you are hungry, however, you might prefer to drop into a *confitería,* a sort of tea shop, to sample a *salteña.* Salteñas, meat patties typical of Bolivia, come in two types, hot and juicy in the morning, and dry and crisper in the afternoon.

Next you turn right up a street called Loayza. Be careful, for the slope is steep and the cobblestones so well polished from wear they are almost as slippery as glass. (Some streets

even have handrails for safety's sake.) Here you will find sou-
venir shops and jewelry shops, or *joyerías,* specializing in silver
objects such as bracelets, rings, and brooches, and decorative
fish made of linked sections so they are flexible.

You climb higher, turn left, and soon you emerge onto
Plaza Murillo, named for Pedro Domingo Murillo, a martyr to
the cause of Bolivian independence who was executed on this
site in 1810. Around this plaza, or square, are the main government buildings of La Paz: the Legislative Palace, where the
Congress meets; the Palacio Quemado, the presidential palace,
with its sentinels standing stiffly in their red uniforms. In
front of this building, one day in 1946, the body of former
president Gualberto Villarroel, slain during a revolution, was
hung from a lamp post by an infuriated mob.

Next to the Palacio Quemado stands the Cathedral of La
Paz, started in 1835 on the site where an earlier church collapsed. Because it is built on such a steep slope, the rear walls
extend thirty-six feet below the level of the front entrance,
and the foundations, in fact, are said to extend all the way to
the level of the Choqueyapu River. Still missing its two towers,
the Cathedral, nevertheless, is an impressive building, with an
immense interior, richly adorned altars, and six rows of massive pillars supporting the roof.

Not far away is the Museo Nacional del Arte, the National
Art Museum. Formerly a colonial residence allowed to fall into
decay, it has been restored to its former splendor. From between marble-arched galleries, you can gaze down into the
quiet interior patio with its famous fountain of glowing alabaster, quarried near Lake Titicaca.

The house where Murillo once lived is not far away, on a
narrow street called Calle Jean. It, too, has been restored to its

colonial charm, with its iron-grilled windows and latticed balcony, and turned into a museum of history and folklore.

Now it is time to return to your hotel. You go past the flower market, a mass of colors from ranked bunches of gladioli, roses, chrysanthemums, and the crimson *kantuta,* the bell-shaped national flower of Bolivia. You make your way down a steep street and then turn left into Avenida Camacho. Your eyes travel upward, past hanging signs of tourist agencies and airlines, still upward until you are looking incredulously at the astonishing sight of Illimani. A veil of mist trails from its lofty peak, forever covered with snow.

In La Paz itself, however, it seldom gets cold enough to snow. But during one great storm around 1610, so much fell that the roof of San Francisco Church fell in. Beginning in 1744, it was rebuilt, and today it is considered a fine example of what is called the hybrid style, or Spanish architecture with variations added by local workmen.

Downtown La Paz is by no means all there is to see in La Paz. You will certainly want to visit some of the finer residential neighborhoods, or *barrios,* with their more elaborate homes. The way to do so is by taxi, but don't be surprised if your driver stops on the way to pick up other passengers headed in the same direction. That is the custom in Bolivia, and a very practical one it is in a country where taxis are not plentiful.

Your first stop might be Monticulo Park, in Sopocachi, with its fine overlook view of the city from beneath the feathery leaves of its eucalyptus grove. Then you head *río abajo,* or downriver, as the paceños say, to the districts of Miraflores, Obrajes, and La Florida. (La Paz has grown downhill, as well as up the slopes to spill over onto the altiplano.) On your way, you pass many fine homes, surrounded by shrubs and flowers, and Bolivia's national police academy. La Florida is almost the end of the paved highway except for Calacoto Park, where working-class families come by bus to spend Sundays. There are food stands with huge legs of roast pork to make sandwiches for those who do not bring their own picnic lunches. At the edge of the park runs the Choqueyapu River, a muddy stream the color of fresh cement that rushes furiously after the city's brief but heavy rains.

No visit to La Paz would be complete, however, without a trip to the Valley of the Moon, and the name describes the type of landscape you will find there. You go beyond Calacoto Park, on a road that skirts Mallasilla Golf Club, the highest course with green fairways in the world. The road climbs, and soon you are winding through an area of fantastic shapes, peaks and pinnacles, holes and columns—and not a single blade or leaf of green. Like the badlands of the Dakotas, the valley presents a panorama of dun-colored earth, too hard for anything to grow, but carved by rains into unbelievable formations.

Here, in this weird and forbidding terrain, you may not exactly be on the moon. But you certainly feel yourself distant from anything that reminds you of human life. You want to get back to La Paz and to see more of Bolivia. But before you set forth again, you will want to learn something of Bolivia's history.

# 3

## Before the Spaniards Came

A dozen miles from the southern end of Lake Titicaca, about two hours' driving distance from La Paz, stand the ruins of Tiahuanaco, the oldest architectural remains in the Americas. Some crumbling terraces, a row of monolithic pillars, two rectangular gateways, a sunken patio with stone jaguar heads staring from its polished walls—these remnants, in part restored, are all that is left of the center of a great civilization that predated the fabled Incas by many centuries. Fortress or temple, palace or marketplace, no one is certain which of these purposes the original structures served, or whether it was all of them at the same time. Where their builders came from, and what happened to them, is also shrouded in mystery.

One thing is sure, however. These silent remains, on a slight rise that was probably an island before Lake Titicaca's waters began to recede, are the traces of a remarkable people. One marvels at their skill in fitting different-shaped blocks of stone together so closely that no cracks were left to fill with mortar. Some of the blocks were held together with tongue-and-groove arrangements carved into the stone with bronze tools or secured with copper pins and clamps. The monumental lintel of the Gate of the Sun, situated at one corner of the vast platform known as the Kalasasaya and the larger of Tiahuanaco's two stone archways (the other arch, a short distance away, is the Gate of the Moon), weighs many tons. Through its opening one can gaze out across the altiplano to the present-day village of Tiahuanaco and Lake Titicaca beyond.

But where did such massive stones come from? There are

Present-day Tiahuanaco is the site of a lively open-air market, set up in the square before the church.

no formations of similar basalt and sandstone within miles of Tiahuanaco. And without knowledge of the wheel, with no beasts of burden larger than the llama, lacking nearby trees with trunks large enough to be used as rollers, how did workmen transport huge blocks weighing as much as four hundred tons to the building site, and then raise them in place? Unfortunately, the Tiahuanacans—like the Incas who succeeded them—had no written language that might have provided a clue, and any word-of-mouth accounts of their history had died out by the time the Spanish conquerors arrived. The only explanation offered by the Indians was a legend relating that Tiahuanaco sprang into being overnight as the home of powerful giants or gods.

Whatever the truth, archeologists place the birth of the Tiahuanaco civilization somewhere between 150 and 450 B.C. It prospered and declined through at least five distinct periods, and at its zenith around A.D. 500 had spread over most of Peru and Bolivia and south as far as central Chile. Pottery of the Tiahuanaco "classic" period has turned up throughout the Andes. It is admired for its purity of lines, in contrast with some of the fancier Inca pottery with double spouts and shapes that resemble animal and human heads. Its characteristic condor and jaguar motifs in reddish browns and black found their way into the earthenware of other early South American cultures.

Scientists place the disappearance of the Tiahuanaco civilization sometime between A.D. 800 and 1200. The cause is unknown, but many believe the end came with a dramatic change in the climate, ruinous to agriculture, wrought by a cataclysmic drop in the water level of Lake Titicaca. And if Tiahuanaco was indeed an island, the disappearance of the surrounding water as the lake shrank could have made it more vulnerable to attackers, possibly from the emerging Inca dynasty.

The Tiahuanaco peoples were certainly not the first to inhabit the bleak altiplano, or *puna,* as it is called in neighboring Peru. The original settlers were most likely hunters, descendants of Asian peoples believed to have crossed to North America via the Bering Straits, perhaps at the end of the Ice Ages when an actual bridge may have existed between the two continents. Gradually, these people spread southward from Alaska, through the rest of North America and into Central America, reaching South America as early as fifteen thousand years ago. As they migrated, they developed through succeeding generations types of agriculture suitable to the regions in which they settled. In Bolivia, remnants of what may have been these earliest people still survive in the primitive Uros fishermen around Lake Poopó, south of Titicaca, and the Chipayas, a small tribe who still wear the type of dress forced upon them by Spanish missionaries in the 1500s.

Besides this theory of immigration from the north, there are other versions to account for the peopling of the Andes. One holds that Indians from the jungles to the east made their way up onto the altiplano and stayed there, but there is very little evidence to bear out this supposition. Another theory seems to have more support. According to this one, the west coast of South America was reached by people from Polynesia or other islands who crossed the Pacific on rafts. Indeed, Thor Heyerdahl with his voyage aboard the *Kon-Tiki* (named, incidentally, after one of the stone idols of Tiahuanaco) proved that such a windborne crossing is possible. Some archeologists see a similarity between the large statues found near Tiahuanaco and the famous sculptured heads of Easter Island in the Pacific. Probably the first immigrants to South America did not come sailing across the Pacific, but it seems likely that others did later, adding their contribution to the cultures that developed there, including the Tiahuanacan.

Perhaps the Aymaras, one of the two main Indian races now living in the Bolivian highlands, are descendants of the lost Tiahuanacan peoples. These dour, stolid folk, darker than their neighbors, the more cheerful Quechuas, were never fully absorbed into the later Inca culture, which also may have sprouted first in Bolivia. At least, legend attributes the Incas' original home to an island in Titicaca, called the Island of the Sun. There the Lord Creator Viracocha fashioned a race of people from clay. Among them were Manco Capac, destined to be the first Inca, and his sister Mama Ocllo, who became his wife. At the command of the Sun God, they set out to found a new home for their people at a spot where the golden staff carried by Manco Capac sank into the earth of its own weight. This occurred at Cuzco, in the heart of what today are the Peruvian highlands.

For anyone who has read or studied about Peru, the rise and fall of the Inca civilization is a familiar story, unexcelled in its telling by the American historian William Prescott in his *Conquest of Peru*. The original tribe ruled by the Incas, a word that actually means "kings," were probably Quechua-speaking. At any rate the Incas made Quechua the official language throughout their empire. These people prospered around Cuzco, gradually enlarging their territory by peaceful means and by war until the Incas ended up dominating the entire Andean region from northern Ecuador south into Chile and Argentina, as well as long stretches of the Pacific coast. At the height of their power the Incas held an area four times larger than the realm of the Egyptian pharaohs, stretching two thousand miles from north to south. The Inca empire was divided into four parts, or *suyos,* and the one that included present-day Bolivia was called the Kollasuya. That is why the Bolivian highland peoples even today are called *kollas,* or *collas,* and the word in various spellings recurs over and over again in place names.

To control their subjects, the Incas built a remarkable system of highways or wide paths crisscrossing the cordilleras, with offshoots down to the coast. Sometimes the roads ran through tunnels or crossed deep gorges on hanging bridges made of vines, which the Spaniards found could support a platoon of soldiers. Along them relays of swift runners, called *chasquís,* sped the orders of the Inca in Cuzco or delivered reports from his lieutenants, enabling the Inca to shuffle his troops to counter threats or put down rebellions anywhere in the empire within a few days. Also, it is said, speedy carriers could rush fish from the Pacific Ocean up to the Inca for him to eat the same day they were caught. To help them stand the pace, the chasquís chewed the leaves of the coca plant, which is cultivated extensively in the Bolivian yungas. Chewed with lime, the leaves form a juice that acts as a sort of pep pill, enabling users to endure long hours of tedious work with little rest. Coca leaves are on sale in the ferias of present-day Bolivia and Peru. Strangely, the use of the drug cocaine, refined from the juice of the coca, is practically unknown among the Andean peoples.

To solidify their power, the Inca kings often transferred conquered tribes to other parts of the empire, settling more trusted subjects in their place. Princes and other highborn persons were brought to Cuzco and given important posts, although their role was clearly that of hostages. Children of vanquished nobles were brought up in the courts of Cuzco and married into royal families, thus taking their place within the Inca society.

This society was a rigid one, in which everyone knew his place. The lot of the common man was to provide food, clothing, utensils, weapons, and warriors in strict obedience to the wishes of the Incas. These and their families governed, and led armies into battle. The priests, whose chief was the reigning Inca, foretold the future by examining the entrails of animals, and they watched the stars and the shadows cast by the

Coca leaves, which the Indians chew to combat fatigue, are sold at open-air markets.

sun to announce the arrival of each season. Their observations enabled them to work out a remarkably accurate calendar of twelve months of three ten-day weeks each, plus one short five-day week, to fit the solar year. This calendar established the pattern for the daily lives of the people. Planting, harvesting, marketing—all followed in rigorous order, accompanied by holiday celebrations and religious ceremonies. During festivals such as Kapak Raymi, held in December to implore the storm god Thunupa to keep the heavy rains from washing out newly sprouted seedlings, richly clad dancers performed to the weird music of wooden flutes and stringed instruments called *charangos* made by stretching cords over empty armadillo shells.

The foundation of the Inca society was the *ayllú,* a community in which members were all related as in a clan. Land was held in common by an ayllú instead of being divided up among individual owners. A remarkable system of terrace building was developed which enabled the Indians to use steep slopes to grow food. The stone-walled terraces were filled with soil from river valleys which was carried up by basketfuls. Farmers had to give a third of their crops to the government for its own use, and another third went into storage to meet the needs of villages beset by crop failures. The government's share permitted the Incas to maintain their vast armies and finance conquests, to construct fortresses in the remotest parts of the empire, and to build cities with fine palaces. In Cuzco, as in Tiahuanaco, walls of stone blocks fit so snugly that not even a knife blade can be thrust between them.

Besides architecture and engineering, the talents of the peoples ruled by the Incas found outlets in pottery making and a variety of other crafts. Gold and silversmiths wrought fine vessels and delicate jewelry for the use of the nobles. Precious metals were not considered to have any intrinsic value but were simply used, like rare woods, to make useful and beautiful objects. Artisans were skilled at weaving (cotton from the warmer coastal plains and wool from the highlands). Articles of clothing included the *chusma*, a sort of poncho with its sides sewn up to the armpits, used by the men, and the ankle-length skirts and *lliclas*, shawls, worn by the women. Of course,

Bolivian weavers still turn llama wool into ponchos on primitive looms.

noble families wore fancier clothing to suit their higher status. The Incas themselves each had several different robes, and capes made of feathers of dazzling hues. Their battle dress included helmets decorated with wavy plumes from birds found only in the eastern jungles.

There is evidence that the practice of medicine was brought to a high level under the Incas. Remedies included quinine, extracted from the cinchona plant, as well as ipecac, balsam, and other herbs that are still sometimes utilized in modern medicine. It is said that their physicians or surgeons were able to perform successful brain operations!

Despite their sophistication, however, the Inca peoples never developed a written language, in which their history could be recorded. But they did make use of a device called the *quipo,* a group of knotted strings of different colors, which helped convey statistical information. For example, a blue string twisted with red thread and knotted in three places might have meant three battalions of enemy warriors or three loads of corn or coca leaves. Since no one today can "read" those quipos now preserved in museums, their meanings remain hidden.

Most of what we know about the history of the Inca civilization comes from Garcilaso de la Vega, born in Cuzco in 1539, the son of a Spanish conquistador and an Inca princess. According to his book, *Royal Commentaries of the Incas*, the Inca dynasty had only thirteen rulers in all in a period of about 250 years. After Manco Capac founded Cuzco, his son Capac Yupanqui pushed its influence south and east. Yahuar Huáscar, faced with a rebellion, fled to the higher altitude around Titicaca, leaving Cuzco to be defended successfully by his son and successor, Inca Viracocha. Greatest of all the Incas, according to Garcilaso, was Pachacuti, who became emperor in

1438. Reconquering parts of the empire that had broken away, Pachacuti proved himself an able general and a far-sighted administrator and urban planner. He rebuilt Cuzco into a great city, worthy to be the capital of the mightiest empire ever to rise in the New World.

Magnificent as it was, the Inca civilization had its dark side. Human sacrifice was practiced to appease the Sun God when he became angry or to assure his beneficence toward agriculture or in coming battles. The next to the last Inca, Huayna Capac, was on his deathbed when news of the arrival of the Spaniards was brought to him. When he died, his two hundred wives and servants were slain and buried with him.

By no means, however, were the Incas unfeeling masters. When populations were transferred, care was taken to resettle them in areas at the same altitudes, and fishermen were never removed from the coast. The system of food reserves also showed concern for the people's welfare. In exchange, the Inca's subjects were expected to accept his word unquestioningly in all matters. They found meaning and significance in their lives not through individual efforts and inventiveness but by following the customs and rituals laid out for their stations in a well-ordered and close-knit society. Undoubtedly its very rigidity led to its defeat and utter destruction within a few years at the hands of a bold and crafty band of Spaniards led by a poor but ambitious adventurer, Francisco Pizarro.

# 4

## From Conquest to Nationhood

In Spain's epic conquest of the Andes, the most memorable events occurred in what today is Peru. However, they determined the course of all South America's history, including Bolivia's, and thus are part of the explanation of the way Bolivia is today. After all, Bolivia itself belonged to the Inca empire that the Spaniards ravaged, and for a long time afterward it was part of what was known as Alto Peru, or Upper Peru.

The search for trade routes to spices and other wealth led the Spanish, like their neighbors the Portuguese, to the Americas. The discovery of the New World by Columbus, sailing under the flag of Spain, brought other adventurers closely on his heels. Cortez conquered the Aztec empire in Mexico for Spain. Balboa established Spanish rule over the Isthmus of Panama. Among the first Europeans to settle there was Francisco Pizarro, the son of a poor Spanish army officer.

Stirred by tales of fabulous wealth farther south, Pizarro gave up farming for exploring. In 1524, he and two partners, Diego de Almagro and Father Fernando de Luque, a priest, pooled their resources and set sail in two leaky ships to scout the Pacific coast southward from Panama. First results were meager, but on a second trip they reached the Inca settlement of Tumbes. There they found enough gold to convince them that stories of a mighty kingdom in the mountains farther south were indeed true. And success brought them reinforcements, including Pizarro's three half brothers, Hernando, Juan, and Gonzalo. In 1531, they returned once more to Peru, this time with the blessings and the financial backing of Emperor Charles V of Spain.

Pizarro's timing could not have been better for his purposes—or worse for the future of the Incas. Contrary to the tradition of naming a single successor, Inca Huayna Capac on his deathbed had bequeathed his empire to two sons. The southern part, administered from Cuzco, went to Huáscar, the Inca's son by his sister-wife. The rest he left to his favorite son Atahualpa, whose mother was the queen of Quito. This division nurtured jealousy and fear in the two half brothers. Huáscar tried to bring the younger Atahualpa under his thumb, but the latter refused to acknowledge Huáscar's authority and instead defeated him in a great battle at Quepaipa in 1532, just when Pizarro and his men were reaching Peru for the third time.

To consolidate his power, Atahualpa ordered hundreds of Huáscar's lieutenants and followers put to death, thereby generating a fatal legacy of hatred within the Inca ranks. Thanks largely to this split, a handful of Spanish adventurers were able to overcome and finally devastate one of the world's truly great civilizations.

How it was done certainly constitutes a black page in history. Brave, enterprising, willing to endure incredible hardships, the Spanish invaders were also capable of treachery and cruelty, which they used without scruples to conquer and then control a people that had welcomed them to their shores as semigods.

Pizarro was building a fort on the Puira River when he got word of the struggle between Huáscar and Atahualpa. Resolving to test the latter, he sent word that he was on his way to pay the Inca a visit. Scaling the mountains through tortuous passes, the Spanish contingent of 177 men and 67 horses reached the fortress-city of Cajamarca just at a time when Atahualpa was resting at an elaborate system of thermal baths nearby. Pizarro dispatched a small detachment to call on the emperor. Clad in their flashing armor, they terrified the Indians as they charged up on their horses, strange beasts never before seen in those parts. Atahualpa, however, did not even deign to receive them. Coolly he sent word that he himself would return the visit the following day.

Back in Cajamarca, there was a moment of panic among the Spaniards at the thought that the haughty Inca and his horde of warriors would soon be on their way. But Pizarro unfolded his plan: He and his men would hide among the buildings and ambush the Inca as he entered the walled city. They would seize and hold him for a ransom that included their own lives. Such a scheme had worked for Cortez against the Aztec emperor Montezuma, and surely it could succeed again.

Indeed it did. Atahualpa arrived borne on a golden litter and accompanied by five thousand of his men. Pizarro's forces fell upon them, muskets blazing. Atahualpa's soldiers staggered back in astonishment, and Pizarro himself had to ward off a blow aimed by one of his men at Atahualpa to keep the Inca from being killed.

Demoralized by the loss of their lord, the Indian warriors withdrew, fearful that further resistance might endanger Atahualpa's life. Thus in a single battle, in which Pizarro alone of the Spaniards was injured, the conquistadores had struck a deathblow at the mighty Empire of the Sun.

Aware that gold was what the Spanish sought above all, Atahualpa now offered to buy his freedom. In exchange, he would fill his cell—measuring 22 by 17 feet—as high as he could reach with gold, and a smaller room nearby with silver for good measure. Pizarro agreed, and for nine months packtrains with precious objects from all over the Inca kingdom streamed into Cajamarca. Meanwhile, Huáscar tried to thwart his half brother by promising the Spanish even greater booty if they would hand Atahualpa over to him to be killed. But Atahualpa learned of the plot and sent messengers to Cuzco with word to have Huáscar done away with, which was accomplished by drowning.

Finally Atahualpa's pledge was fulfilled. Before the Spaniard's eyes lay a treasure in gold that would be worth $15 million today, waiting to be melted down and divided, with the royal fifth to be set aside for King Charles of Spain. Now Pizarro was in a quandary. Could Atahualpa be trusted if he were released? Or would his subjects rally to his support and slay the Spaniards? For Pizarro, who some say had grown to admire his adversary in captivity, these were weighty questions. Isolated and so few in numbers as the Spaniards were, however, there could really be little doubt about the decision. Atahualpa must die. He asked whether his end might be made easier if he were to accede to Friar Vicente de Valverde's pleas and turn Christian. Yes, he was told, and was promptly baptized with the name Juan, or John. Then, instead of being burned at the stake, he was strangled with a rope around his neck.

Now the great Inca was gone and nothing seemed to stand in the Spaniards' way—except their own jealousies and suspicions. A long quarrel between Francisco Pizarro and his partner Almagro dragged on for years. After a fruitless overland journey of two thousand miles to Chile and back, looking for plunder, Almagro was slain. And Pizarro, the mighty conqueror himself, met the same fate he had dealt out to Atahualpa. One night as he returned to his sumptuous home in Lima, the "City of the Kings," which he founded in 1535, he was seized and strangled by a band of Almagro's bitter followers.

News of the bickering and deadly rivalry among the conquerors upset King Charles so much that he sent his own lieutenants or viceroys to govern Peru. Gradually the viceroys brought order and established a form of colonial government, consisting of viceroyalties and *audiencias,* the latter meaning a place where a court met to hear and rule on complaints. Most of what today is Bolivia was organized as the Audiencia of Charcas, under the control of the Viceroy of Peru in Lima,

Dancers at the Oruro carnival perform the traditional *Waca,* in which they imitate the bullfights of the Spanish conquerors.

and for a time the Viceroyalty of La Plata in Buenos Aires. The viceroyalties were ruled from Madrid by the Council of the Indies, which appointed the viceroys and other officials in the New World and encouraged settlement and farming.

Along with their technology, the Spaniards brought to their new realms in South America a system of landholding that had proved successful in other parts of their empire. Land was divided and parceled out as *encomiendas* among persons who had rendered services to the crown or had means for developing the new territories. For example, Pizarro's half brother Gonzalo received a large encomienda in Charcas, today the Bolivian department, or state, of Chuquisaca. To work their encomiendas, the Spaniards borrowed from the Incas a system of forced labor called the *mita*. Under the Incas, subjects of the emperors could be drafted to work at certain tasks, such as raising crops or building roads or cities, for specific periods only. In the hands of the Spaniards, however, the mita became a thinly disguised form of full-time slavery. The Indians were considered part of an encomienda's natural wealth, just as much as the plants or animals or minerals found on it, and they were rounded up in hunts like cattle to supply labor for field, orchard, or mine.

Periodically the Indians rebelled against this treatment in bloody uprisings. José Gabriel Condorcanqui, a descendent of the Inca Tupac Amaru, whose name he borrowed, took his complaints of injustice all the way to the Spanish court in Madrid. But the ill-treatment continued, and in 1780 he led a revolt. Seizing and hanging the governor of Tinta, Province of Cuzco, he declared himself the Inca. An army of seventeen thousand men from Buenos Aires crossed the Andes and stamped out the rebellion, but in another outbreak Tupac Amaru's brother laid siege to the town of Sorata at the foot of

Mount Illampu in Bolivia. There he had a dam built on a river and then opened it suddenly to flood the town.

The Catholic Church and the Spanish Crown itself attempted to halt the abuses against the Indians, but these efforts were generally ignored and deeply resented by the American-born white, or largely white, residents of Spanish America, called Creoles. In fact, they complained that Madrid and its representatives paid little heed to their own grievances, that the best jobs in the colonies always went to those born in Spain, that Spain acted in its own interests and not those of its colonies. Like the English colonists in North America, the Creoles and the *mestizo*, or mixed, population felt they were saddled with arbitrary taxes and unfair restrictions on trade. Their pride was irked by the notion prevalent in the colonies that only things from Spain had any real value. To the Indians, most of them virtually slaves, it made no difference who ruled them.

Gradually these feelings led to desires for independence. The first stirrings came in the late eighteenth century when British and French marauders bagan to raid the South American coastline. With them came new ideas from Europe and from North America. The French emperor Napoleon's war with Spain weakened the mother country, and revolts began to erupt in its South American colonies, in Venezuela in 1808 and in Peru in 1809.

Bolivia's turn also came in 1809. With the arrest in Charcas—today the city of Sucre—of two brothers charged with conspiring, the *chuquisaqueños,* as the people of Chuquisaca province were called, rose in revolt. The news soon reached La Paz, where it excited the imagination of a young lawyer, Pedro Domingo Murillo. He and a dozen other men began to plot against the government. Seizing the governor and the bishop of La Paz, they set up a fifteen-man *junta,* or board, to govern the province. But their movement was short-lived. With the help of five hundred soldiers from Buenos Aires, the authorities loyal to Spain arrested and hanged Murillo and eight of his companions, who thenceforth were known as the Nine Proto-Martyrs. On their way to the gallows, Murillo prophesied: "No one will be able to put out the torch I have lit!"

Soon all of Spain's colonies in South America were aflame in a vast struggle for independence. Among the leaders were Manuel Belgrano and San Martín in Argentina, José Artigas

Pedro Domingo
Murillo.

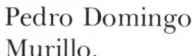

in Uruguay, and Bernardo O'Higgins in Chile. Belgrano was
defeated in a series of battles in Bolivia, but, uniting their
forces under Simón Bolívar, the colonists finally managed to
liberate Gran Colombia—today the countries of Venezuela,
Colombia, and Ecuador. Then, in 1824, Bolívar dispatched an
army under General Sucre from Trujillo in Peru over the
Andes to meet the loyalist forces of the Spanish general Can-
terac. At dusk at the town of Junín, near Cuzco, in hand-to-
hand combat in which not a shot was fired, Sucre's men
routed the loyalist army, and in a second great battle at Ayacu-
cho defeated an avenging Spanish force that outnumbered
them two to one. Now Sucre marched south to the region
known as Upper Peru, where he overcame the remaining
Spanish troops under General Olañeta. On August 6, 1825,
representatives of the five provinces of Upper Peru—La Paz,
Potosí, Chuquisaca, Cochabamba, and Santa Cruz—met at
Charcas to create a new nation to be called Bolivia, after Bolívar. They offered Bolívar the presidency, but "The Liberator
of South America," as he was known, declined. However, he
agreed to help write a constitution, adoped in May, under
which Sucre assumed the presidency.

# 5

## Bolivia Since Independence

The Bolivians were united in their desire for independence, but since they attained it the art of self-government has seemed almost beyond their reach. Except for a few brief periods, the country has never enjoyed political stability. Since its birth, Bolivia has had a new president, on the average, every two and a half years, and not more than a handful managed to last out their terms. In the early days especially, most were ousted by rivals ambitious for power and a chance to make themselves rich. In more modern times, social philosophy and economic disparities have become important factors in the rapid changes of government. But whatever the causes, it is amply clear that the impatient Bolivians have not yet learned—or perhaps never even cared to learn—the practice of "consensus politics," in which a majority of the people accept certain principles and goals and agree to follow a set of rules for bringing about orderly change.

In the first flush of enthusiasm over independence, the country got off to a good start. Born in Venezuela like Bolívar, President Antonio José de Sucre received wide support from the people, who renamed the city of Charcas in his honor. He ordered a census taken, established public schools,

Antonio José de Sucre.

and encouraged immigration from Germany and other European nations. But troubles soon began to mount. Constitutional provisions for protecting the Indians and improving their lot were never applied. Provincial governors refused to send their tax contributions to the federal treasury. The bickerings and jealousies that prevailed throughout the Andean countries from the earliest days of conquest broke out anew.

In its first seventy-five years, Bolivia was governed by a series of strong-man leaders called *caudillos*. Most were generals, since in a country without a strong tradition of civilian leadership the army is a convenient springboard to politics. They came and went in dreary succession, often departing with large amounts of public funds. During this sorry period of turmoil, armed rebellions and guerrilla uprisings constantly broke out, governments were overthrown, and six presidents were assassinated in office. Two years after he left office, Sucre himself was shot to death in Quito, Ecuador, while returning from an unsuccessful peacemaking mission to Venezuela for his friend, Bolívar. It was not until 1855 that Bolivia got its first president elected directly by the people.

One of Bolivia's better early presidents was General Andrés Santa Cruz, a lieutenant of Sucre's, who founded art and trade schools, and universities in both La Paz and Cochabamba. One of the worst was Manuel Isidoro Belzú, who governed under a reign of terror. Opponents were killed or sent away to rot in jungle outposts. Belzú once insulted the British ambassador and was said to have sent him out of La Paz riding backward on a donkey. This act so outraged England's Queen Victoria, according to a tale that is probably not entirely true, that she instructed the British fleet to fire on Bolivia. When told this could not be done, she ordered the country stricken from her map! Later, when threatened with insurrection, Belzú resigned and went into exile, with the pronouncement that Bolivia was ungovernable.

Probably Bolivia's most disastrous president was General Mariano Malgarejo, a tyrant who ruled the country with an iron fist from 1865 to 1870. Described by one Bolivian writer as an "innate criminal," Melgarejo was said during one drunken fit to have ordered a squad of soldiers to march out a second-story window to demonstrate their loyalty. He sold land belonging to the Indians and put the money in his own pocket. His incompetence in foreign affairs cost the country thousands of square miles of territory. In return for the right to send boats down the Amazon River, he ceded a rubber-rich jungle region to Brazil, and he signed a treaty with Chile so vague that it left ownership of nitrate deposits along the Pacific coast in doubt, leading to a war in 1879 between Chile on the one hand and Bolivia and Peru on the other. As a result of this conflict, in which most of the fighting involved naval vessels, Peru and Bolivia between them lost four of their provinces. Although the lost territory was mostly desert, it was rich in minerals, especially borax and nitrates, the latter an important element in fertilizers. And with the land lost in the "Nitrate War," as it was called, went Bolivia's only stretch of seacoast.

In the wrangle over peace terms that followed, the American secretary of state, James G. Blaine, tried to persuade Chile to give up its territorial gains. Talks among the contestants were held aboard the American cruiser *Lackawanna,* anchored off the coast of Chile. The Chileans refused to relinquish their gains, but they did agree to build a railroad from Arica on the coast to La Paz and to guarantee the Bolivians the right to use it without paying customs charges on shipments of goods.

Bolivia has never recovered from its humiliation at the hands of Chile, or officially acknowledged the loss of its provinces, the subject of heated discussion even today. Patriotic groups meet regularly in Bolivia to keep the issue alive. As recently as 1974, the Bolivian government sought to reopen talks with Chile and Peru on the matter.

However, the construction of the Arica–La Paz railroad, making it easier for Bolivia to ship its minerals to the world and import other products in return, helped initiate a period of economic boom. A second railroad linking the mining center of Oruro in the highlands to the Chilean port of Antofagasta was completed when Bolivia's president Aniceto Acre hammered in the last spike in 1892. Roads and bridges and other public works were constructed, and steamships, brought up piece by piece from the coast and then reassembled, began to ply Lake Titicaca. La Paz mushroomed into a busy commercial city, with streetcars and a public lighting system and even small industries. It was about this time that La Paz gained recognition as Bolivia's real, or de facto, capital rather than sleepy, aristocratic Sucre.

This period was also one of relative political stability, known as the "Age of Silver" because President Acre and his three successors were the wealthy owners of silver mines. Tin, however, rapidly replaced silver as Bolivia's most important mineral and became the basis of sudden prosperity. Prospectors flocked in from all over the world, and great fortunes were made.

This peaceful progress was interrupted by the second of the two wars Bolivia engaged in with neighboring countries. This one was fought against Paraguay in 1933. As in the war with Chile, both access to the sea and wealth that presumably lay underground were reasons for the strife. At issue was control of a huge tract known as the Chaco, or more specifically, the western part called the Chaco Boreal, which belonged to Bolivia.

Probably few parts of the world could be found less worth fighting over, for the Chaco is an unpromising area of sagebrush and chaparral that turns swampy during the rains. From time to time, great hordes of locusts swarm over the land eating every leaf and blade of grass in their path. But for Bolivia—bereft of ports on the Pacific—the Chaco Boreal was the gateway to the Atlantic, via two rivers, the Paraguay and its tributary the Pilcomayo, which formed its borders. The Paraguayans, on the other hand, were interested in the Chaco for its quebracho, a treelike shrub that yields tannin, a substance used in tanning leather. Besides, oil had been discovered in the eastern Bolivian lowlands by an American petro-

La Casa de la Libertad, Sucre—Bolivia's Independence Hall.

leum company, and both the Bolivians and the Paraguayans were convinced that more deposits could be found in the Chaco.

Trouble started when the Bolivians, to protect their access to the Atlantic, began to build forts along the Pilcomayo. As fast as they did so, the Paraguayans pushed a string of forts north up the Paraguay. Soon both nations were manning small fortified outposts at various points throughout the

Chaco Boreal. A series of raids and skirmishes led in 1933 to the outbreak of full-scale warfare, in which Bolivia's soldiers were at a considerable disadvantage. Most of them came from the altiplano and were not used to the hot climate of the low-lying Chaco. Besides, they were fighting miles from their bases, while the Paraguayans' sources of supplies were close at hand.

The fighting went mostly in favor of the Paraguayans, and it lasted for more than a year. When it was over, fifty thousand Bolivian and forty thousand Paraguayan soldiers had lost their lives. Bolivia had to surrender $10 million worth of arms and the Chaco Boreal to Paraguay. Oil never was found in the Chaco, and today quebracho and cattle remain the area's only products of any great value.

In one important way, however, the war was a turning point for Bolivia. It ushered in a new era of social and political change. Shocked and humbled by their country's poor showing against Paraguay, a group of younger officers rose to leadership in the army, bent on reform. Nationalist and socialist in outlook, they took most of their political ideas from Europe, especially Germany, Italy, and Russia, which were going through a period of social upheaval. The new breed of Bolivian military men were deeply troubled by their country's backwardness, for which they blamed the oligarchy of wealthy mining barons and landowners. Tin mining, the backbone of Bolivia's economy, was already becoming less and less profitable, and the young officers now in power and their intellectual supporters were convinced that the mining companies and their foreign stockholders were at fault. The government ordered the mine owners to turn their foreign currency earnings over to the national treasury in exchange for bolivianos, and it took over the oil company formed by Standard Oil, the

American company that had discovered petroleum in Bolivia's Oriente. Then the new radical leaders began to think about breaking up the large farms into plots to be distributed among the small-scale Indian farmers.

All these measures quickly drew support from Bolivia's middle-class cholo workers and impoverished Indians, now dignified by the term *campesinos*—peasants—but they brought the new leaders into conflict with the older, conservative military officials and the mine- and landowning classes. Their opposition so thwarted one president, Germán Busch Becerra, that he committed suicide while in office in 1939. The reform efforts of the nationalists were also hampered by the worldwide economic depression of the 1930s. Their sympathies with Fascist Italy and Nazi Germany complicated matters further. In fact, with the outbreak of World War II, the United States and Germany became active rivals for influence over the Bolivians. The German colony, abetted by German agents, worked openly to swing Bolivia to the side of the Axis powers. However, the Americans managed to persuade Bolivian president Enrique Peñaranda to confiscate Lloyd Aereo Boliviano, a German-owned airline that formed part of the Nazis' transcontinental airway system in South America, and in 1943 Bolivia entered the war on the side of the United States and its allies.

This move proved unpopular with the army because of the sympathies of many of its officers with Germany and its brand of national socialism. Ousting Peñaranda in a bloodless coup, the military installed an army major, Gualberto Villarroel, as president. Villarroel sought to extend social reforms, but his harsh methods so outraged the public that a bloody revolt broke out. A mob stormed right into the presidential palace, shot the president, and hurled his body into Plaza Murillo, where it was hanged from a lamp post. Over 250 persons died in the fighting that raged in La Paz for four days.

During World War II and immediately following, the reform movement in Bolivia was sidetracked, but it soon broke out afresh under the banner of the Movimiento Nacionalista Revolucionario (MNR), or Nationalist Revolutionary Movement, an amalgam of intellectuals and trade union leaders. Campaigning for the presidency from exile in Argentina, the MNR's leader Victor Paz Estenssoro won an election in 1951 but was prevented from taking office by a military junta. In protest, armed miners and workers the following year started a revolt, which succeeded after a week of fierce fighting in the very streets of La Paz. Paz Estenssoro was flown home from Buenos Aires in triumph, and Bolivia entered a period, remarkable in its history, of social change and political stability that lasted for twelve years.

The MNR owed its rise to three men above all others: Paz Estenssoro, his vice-president Hernan Siles Zuazo, and a labor leader named Juan Lechin Oquendo. The bespectacled Paz was an economics professor before he entered politics, and Siles was the son of a former Bolivian president. Lechin headed the miners' union, which he began to organize when he was still in his teens. Handsome and powerfully built, he also played soccer for professional teams, which helped him become so popular that the miners elected him a senator in 1947. But his Marxist political ideas made him feared by Bolivia's conservative forces.

Under the three leaders, the MNR government introduced sweeping reforms. It took over control of the large tin mines, paying their owners $20 million for the properties, and set up a state company, Corporación Minera de Bolivia, known as Comibol, to run them. It extended voting rights to illiterates, thereby enfranchising the Indians, and greatly increased government spending for education. The MNR measure with the greatest social impact, however, was a land reform. The government took over large estates of more than fifteen hundred acres and divided them into smaller plots, which were given to the campesinos, many of whom had already begun to seize large properties and move in as squatters. A separate educational system was set up to accompany the land reform, and for the first time Bolivian Indian children began going to school. Campesinos from the altiplano were encouraged to move to more fertile land in the Oriente. Years later, when Ernesto "Che" Guevara attempted to start a Cuban-style revo-

Indian children with school benches they have made in a carpentry class.

lution among Bolivia's campesinos, they proved loyal to the government, which had guaranteed them the right to own their own land.

The rise to power of the MNR placed United States officials in a quandary. They were skeptical about supporting a movement that had blamed "Yankee imperialism" for most of Bolivia's woes. The seizure of private property struck many Washington officials as communist, and they feared that the MNR leaders, especially Lechin with his Marxist principles, would be unduly influenced by the Soviet Union. Yet, the administration of President Dwight Eisenhower wisely concluded that Paz Estenssoro and his associates were, above all else, reformers seeking social justice and ardent Bolivian nationalists who would not turn to Russia unless they were denied help elsewhere. Large amounts of American financial aid flowed to Bolivia to help the government finance reforms, and in the face of a Russian offer to build a tin smelter for the Bolivians, the United States and West Germany provided technical help to Comibol aimed at increasing output of the tin mines. The United States also paid for construction of a paved road between Santa Cruz and Cochabamba, making it cheaper for farmers in the Oriente to market their produce in the high valleys and on the altiplano.

The MNR brought long overdue social reforms, but it was less successful in solving the country's economic problems. In fact, without the help it received from the United States, it is doubtful whether the MNR would have remained in power as long as it did. Lechin insisted that Comibol hire as many miners as possible—more than were needed, as it turned out. Many of the plots given to the campesinos were so small they could barely produce enough to feed the families that worked them, leaving nothing over to be sold in the markets. In fact, a good number of the campesinos were content simply to live for themselves. More than half of the Indians settled in the Oriente drifted back to their familiar surroundings on the altiplano. Then, too, some of the United States aid measures produced unexpected results. For example, the U.S. government sent large amounts of wheat flour to Bolivia, which undoubtedly improved the diet of many of Bolivia's poor. But because the imported flour was cheaper than that made locally, Bolivia's flour mills had to close, and workers lost their jobs. Meanwhile, prices of everything kept rising in a period of inflation.

After Paz Estenssoro's presidential term ended, his vice-president Siles succeeded him. Paz won a second term in 1960, but already the MNR's unity had been broken and its power had begun to wane. Paz and Lechin, who was now vice-president, quarreled when the former announced plans to transfer some of the excess miners to other jobs and to take other harsh steps to stop prices from climbing. Lechin abandoned the vice-presidency, and revolts broke out in the mines. Many army officers had been irked when Paz gave an American oil company concessions to drill for petroleum. When the army began a rebellion, Paz fled to Lima, and a military junta headed by a General Alfredo Ivando Candia and an air force brigadier, René Barrientos Ortuño, formed a new government.

Barrientos, who ran for president and won in 1966, was a handsome pilot who never lost his passion for flying. He had become an MNR hero in 1952 when he flew the plane that brought Paz home from exile in Argentina, and as president he now pledged himself to carry forward the MNR reforms. He loved to fly around the country, dropping in unexpectedly on Quechua Indian villages and talking to the people in their own language, which he spoke exceedingly well. His personal courage made him popular also. Once when two air force parachutists died in a demonstration because their chutes failed to open, Barrientos—to refute the charges that the military were using faulty equipment—invited newspapermen to select a parachute, took it aloft, and made a safe jump with it that settled the controversy.

Barrientos' popularity stood him in good stead when Che Guevara tried to foster an uprising of campesinos. An Argentine who had helped Fidel Castro organize his successful revolution in the Sierra Maestra mountains of Cuba, Guevara suddenly dropped out of sight, leaving the world wondering whether he had died or gone off to start a revolution somewhere else. The mystery ended when he showed up in Bolivia, where he thought he might duplicate Castro's Cuban feat in the Andes. But the campesinos, always suspicious of strangers, failed to rally to his support, and instead gave information to Barrientos' soldiers that helped them finally track down Che and his band. Most of them died while fighting, but Che was captured and executed.

Barrientos' love of flying brought about his own death not long afterward. While taking off in his helicopter from a soccer stadium near Oruro, he flew into some telephone wires, and his craft fell in flames.

After Barrientos' death, Bolivia's presidency changed hands five times in a span of twenty-eight months. One of the incumbents served only two days before being ousted by General Juan José Torres Gonzales, who ordered some zinc and lead mines taken away from their foreign owners. He also canceled the drilling concession of the Gulf Oil Corporation, which had built a pipeline over the Andes to Chile's port of Arica. These actions won popular support for Torres, but his failure to include power-hungry politicians in his government led to his downfall. In 1971, he was overthrown by a movement headed by Hugo Banzer Suarez, an army colonel in exile in Brazil who was backed by the military, the MNR, and a middle-class party called the Bolivian Socialist Falange.

The Banzer government has devoted much attention to developing Bolivia's resources in the Oriente. It has agreed to sell iron ore to Argentina, and will supply natural gas to Brazil through a pipeline to be built all the way across the continent to São Paulo. In return, Brazil and Argentina will help finance highway and railway construction in eastern Bolivia. By agreeing to pay Gulf Oil for its properties seized by the Torres regime, the government also hopes to attract new foreign investors to the country with funds and technology to develop industry and agriculture. Also, Bolivia has joined the five other Andean countries to form the Andean Common Market, ANCOM, in the expectation that by abolishing customs barriers and allowing goods to move freely from one nation to another a single large market will be created to the benefit of all.

However, Banzer has had a difficult time just staying in power, especially after the MNR withdrew from the government coalition and Paz Estenssoro was forced to go into exile in Argentina again. The Banzer regime has been constantly threatened with plots and attempted coups, and has resorted to authoritarian measures such as curbs on press freedoms and political meetings. It seems clear that Bolivia still has a long distance to travel before it manages to reach a lasting stage of political maturity and stability.

# 6

## Treasures in the Earth

Ask what product France is famous for, and most people will reply perfume or wine. For Argentina, the answer is beef. For Brazil, coffee. And for Bolivia, it is tin. In truth, a good many people know practically nothing else about Bolivia other than the fact that it is a major source of tin.

At one time, nearly all of the tin used by industries throughout the world was mined in the Bolivian highlands. Today most of it comes from Malaysia and other countries in Southeast Asia, but Bolivia still contributes about 20 percent of the world's supply. For almost five centuries tin and other minerals have been the chief source of Bolivia's wealth, as well as the root of many of its woes, as they have for several other Andean nations.

In fact, all the way from Ecuador to Chile, the Andes Mountains are one of the world's great storehouses of mineral riches, and the name *Andes* itself has a sort of mineral origin. It comes from the Indian word *anta*, meaning copper, and for the ancient Inca civilization copper was much more important than the gold and silver so prized by the Spaniards.

Through the centuries, treasure wrested from the Andes has produced fabulous wealth, but little of it remained in the hands of Bolivia and its neighbors. In the colonial days, gold and silver by the tons were hauled away in Spanish galleons, going first to Panama, where the bullion was borne by muleback across the isthmus, and then aboard other vessels sailing in armed convoys across the Atlantic to the ports of Spain. The Spanish treasury used these riches to finance wars and conquests and to pay for manufactured articles imported from England, Holland, France, and other countries. There the doubloons and other Spanish coins that flooded through Europe helped end the system of barter economy and set the Western world along the course to modern-day capitalism.

Then came the Industrial Revolution, opening markets for all sorts of metals used in manufacturing. In the last century, the process of preserving food in cans was discovered, suddenly making Bolivia's tin a valuable commodity. Tin made vast fortunes for a few, the handful of Bolivian families that owned the mines and the foreign companies that did the refining. But by the time the Bolivian government itself got around to taking over and running the mines, the richest deposits had been exhausted, and mining was becoming less and less profitable.

Nonetheless, four-fifths of Bolivia's exports today are mineral products, with tin constituting the largest portion by far. Silver, tungsten, antimony, lead, zinc, bismuth, and copper are also exported, as is petroleum. Now Bolivia is beginning to ship iron ore from mines in the eastern lowlands to nearby Argentina. In short, mining is still the backbone of Bolivia's economy and is likely to remain so for some time.

Some people have even gone so far as to claim that without mining there would be no Bolivia. Yet others argue that mining has been a mixed blessing for the country at best. It gave enormous political power to a select few—the tin barons before the mines were nationalized, the fifty thousand mine workers afterward. Mining made Bolivia's economy overly dependent on exports and kept the country's attention focused on the barren highlands to the neglect of the rich agricultural region of the Oriente. It helped perpetuate a form of semislavery and condemned thousands of workers to disease-ridden lives under conditions of misery, depicted graphically by the Bolivian writer Augusto Cépedes in *Metal del Diablo,* The Devil's Metal, a novel based on the life of the tin baron Simón Patiño.

In any case, to say that Bolivia exists for the sake of mining is a strange statement, in face of ample evidence that the Incas built a great civilization in the harsh Andean highlands in which mining was of secondary importance only. Theirs was basically an agricultural society, in which amazing architectural talents were employed in building terraces and aqueducts so food could be raised on plunging mountainsides. To be sure, metal was used for both utility and decoration. The Indians mined and smelted copper to make knives and hammers, carpentry tools, tips for the sticks they used to break open the soil, and objects of personal adornment. Ladies in the Inca courts adjusted their hair while watching themselves in mirrors of polished copper, and sometimes entire walls were decorated with copper plating. The Indians learned to harden copper by alloying it with tin to make bronze, from which they fashioned weapons of war and tools for working with stone. Gold and silver, of course, were wrought into beautiful goblets and plates and jewelry, reserved for the nobility. But neither metal was held to have any intrinsic value beyond its use.

Because of their isolation from other advanced civilizations, it is somewhat of a mystery how the early inhabitants of South

Tin ingots ready to be loaded for export.

America became so skilled at working with metals. Probably they observed how veins in certain rocks became soft when placed near hot fires. From there it was a fairly easy step to the melting of copper in vessels made of clay placed over charcoal fires, which the Indians could make red-hot by blowing on the coals through hollow reeds. But it must have taken years of experimenting and trial and error before they stumbled upon a way of reducing silver, which does not fuse as easily as copper. The silver ore had to be pounded with stones or copper hammers, then mixed with a flux of lead sulfide, which the Indians called *soroche,* and finally melted in clay furnaces with holes in them to provide for drafts. These furnaces, called *huairas,* were usually constructed on hillsides to catch the winds. They were fired principally at night, when the winds blow hardest. Early travelers to Bolivia recounted how peaks and steep slopes would glow with as many as fifteen thousand of these primitive furnaces blazing in the darkness.

For the Spaniards, extracting metallic wealth from their colonies in South America was a fairly simple matter. At first they were content merely to strip the Incas of their gold and silver objects and melt them down into ingots for easier transportation. Only after there was no more to loot—within a few years of the Conquest—did they actually bother to think about mining. By bribing and torturing the Indians, the Spaniards soon learned the whereabouts of the mines, even though many Indians preferred to die rather than give up the secrets.

Practically all the mines in operation at the end of the colonial period had been known to the Indians. There was one important exception, however: the fabled *Cerro Rico de Potosí,* or the Rich Mountain of Potosí, discovered in the sixteenth century. Veined throughout with silver, Cerro Rico quite possibly is the richest mine complex of all time, having in four centuries yielded more than one billion dollars' worth of silver. So much silver poured from its mines that *"Vale un Potosí"*—"It's worth a Potosí"—became a byword for wealth throughout Spain's empire. And so widespread did the fame of Potosí become that it even reached faraway China, where the city was known as Pei tu Hsi. "I am Potosí, Treasure of the World, and the Envy of Kings," proclaimed the proud motto on the city's original coat of arms.

Jealous of its richest single possession, Spain kept most foreigners away from Potosí. But occasionally merchants of other nationalities were allowed to settle there, and from time to time travelers passed through who left fascinating accounts of the city in the heydays of its colonial glory.

One such traveler, who visited Potosí on his way from Buenos Aires to Lima in 1658, was Acarete du Biscay, a Frenchman pretending to be the nephew of a Spanish nobleman. In the journal he kept, du Biscay described the churches richly adorned with silver and imported tapestries, sumptuous homes where families always dined from silver dishes placed before them by Indian slaves, gentlemen and ladies who strolled about in clothes of silk and lace. He wrote of a two-week-long *fiesta,* or holiday, celebrating the birth of a Spanish prince, when everyone from officials and tradesmen to miners, goldsmiths, servants, and even Indians, marched in parades and danced at balls. Mock battles were staged between floats representing galleons, with real cannon firing blank charges at an imitation castle. The fight ended with both "ships" and "fortress" going up in flames.

Today little of that sort of excitement stirs Potosí. (Nearly all of the actual fighting during Bolivia's frequent revolutions has occurred in and near La Paz.) As silver mining has declined, so has Potosí's importance to Bolivia. Its population, which one hundred years after its founding in 1545 had grown to around 160,000 to make it the largest city in South America, has shrunk to less than 60,000. To be sure, this hardly makes Potosí a ghost town, but its former brilliance has just about faded away.

One can drive from La Paz to Potosí in about ten hours, on a highway that is paved as far as the tin mining center of Oruro. Another way of getting there, although the journey is longer, is to take the ferrobus, a self-propelled rail car that is a comfortable and popular means of travel wherever one exists in Bolivia. Potosí is very high, about fourteen thousand feet, so warm outer clothing is essential even in summer, although one sheds it quickly if he visits a mine, where the temperature rises rapidly as the *jaula,* or cage, descends the mineshaft.

Looming above the city is the perfect pyramid of Cerro Rico, whose outline appears on many Bolivian coins. There

Oruro is the site of a yearly carnival. Here people are gathering for a parade.

are a number of interesting churches to visit, the oldest dating back to 1555. Most were built in the so-called mestizo style of Spanish architecture with adaptations by local craftsmen, many of them Indians trained by Jesuit priests. Just off the main square, Plaza 10 de Noviembre, stands the Casa de La Moneda, or mint, where Cerro Rico's silver was refined and melted down into ingots or stamped into coins. The building is constructed of brick and stone and massive beams hauled from far away to support the heavy iron and wooden machinery. Today the Casa de la Moneda is a museum, where one can look down from an arched, covered gallery onto a fountain in the quiet patio, or study the collection of paintings by such Bolivian colonial artists as Holguin and Gamarra, and the twentieth-century Potosí painter, Cecilio Guzman de Rojas. On the outskirts of town is the church of San Lorenzo with its famous *portal,* or gateway, of ornately carved wood. And farther away, perhaps another thousand feet higher, is a thermal lake called the Lagoon of the Incas, where one can swim in naturally warm waters while gazing at the fantastic circle of lofty peaks.

Cerro Rico's rivulets of silver are just about exhausted. In fact, more wealth in silver and other minerals is probably being recovered from the huge piles of tailings, refuse rock thrown aside during mining, than the silver still locked in the mountain itself. Tin has long since surpassed silver in importance to Bolivia's economy, and the center of the tin mining industry is Oruro.

Named for the Uro Uros, a tribe of primitive Indians subdued and almost exterminated by the conquering Incas, Oruro is a dry and often dusty city, the color of the surrounding brown soil. Except for a ten-story building or two fronting its pleasant main plaza, the buildings are tile-roofed, one- and two-story affairs in a jumble running down the slope of a hill and sprawling over the level space below. It is easy to get lost here—everything looks so alike. Still, Oruro, with a population of 120,000, is among Bolivia's four most important cities. It is a rail hub, with lines running to La Paz, Cochabamba, the Chilean port of Antofagasta, to Potosí and on to Sucre, and to Jujuy in Argentina and thence all the way to Buenos Aires on the Atlantic.

Around Oruro are Bolivia's most important tin mines. Near Catavi, southeast of Oruro on a line running to Potosí, is the richest complex of them all, discovered by Simón I. Patiño, an uneducated mestizo who became one of the richest men on earth. Patiño was a poor independent miner who from boyhood hacked at the earth with pick and shovel. For years he kept at his back-breaking work, often aided by his wife, certain that one day he would strike a vein that would make his fortune. That day came in 1904 when he stumbled on a deposit of unusual purity, which he kept secret until he could register it as his own. By reinvesting most of his earnings, he gradually added more and more mines to his holdings, which became known as the Llallagua group, for many years the most productive tin complex in the world. One of the mines at Catavi, Siglo XX, or Twentieth Century, alone contains five hundred miles of tunnels and shafts and connecting galleries, and in places is two thousand feet deep.

Patiño's real genius was his ability to understand and put together complicated financial deals. Despised by Bolivia's wealthy aristocracy because of his humble origins and mixed blood, he can hardly be blamed if he flaunted some of his great wealth by building a sumptuous town house in Cochabamba, the city of his birth, and a huge estate on its outskirts. Nevertheless, he spent little time at either of these places, liv-

Miners at work in a tin mine at Catavi.

ing most of his life as a rich man abroad. In fact, he finally merged all his holdings into a company called Patiño Mines & Enterprises Consolidated, Inc., with headquarters in the state of Delaware.

Patiño was the head of one of three Bolivian families who controlled the country's large mines, known as the *gran minería,* accounting for three-fourths of the total tin output. The others were the Hochschilds, a family of German-Chilean descent, and the Aramayos, headed by Carlos Aramayo, who like Patiño was of vigorous Indian-Spanish stock. Since 1952, the Bolivian government has controlled the large mines through

Comibol. But the cordilleras are scarred with hundreds and hundreds of smaller mines, some looking like nothing more than caves in the hillsides. About twenty or thirty are medium-sized mines, in a class called the *minería mediana*. But the rest are almost one-man affairs from which their owners barely manage to scrape a living.

To be really profitable, mining in Bolivia requires huge amounts of capital for transportation equipment and heavy machinery, since the richest veins are generally found in the most inaccessible places, often high up just under the snow line. Usually they run very deep, and the deeper they go the more it costs to pump out the water that seeps in, until a point is reached when mining is no longer profitable.

Until recently, all of Bolivia's tin was refined abroad, most of it in Texas and in Britain. The ore goes out in the form of concentrates; some of the other minerals have been removed by washing and mechanical means and by a process in which mercury is used for carrying away the impurities. Tin is almost always found in association with other minerals that formerly were discarded. Nowadays, such minerals as lead and zinc also have to be utilized if tin mining is to remain profitable. However, little by little, as the richest veins of tin have run out and few new ones have been discovered in their place, the grade of tin—that is, the amount of tin content in the concentrates exported—has dropped lower and lower. Consequently, the prices Bolivia receives for its tin have been going down, too. To help remedy this situation, the government has now built the nation's first tin smelter in Oruro, which from now on will enable it to export tin instead of just concentrates.

The Bolivian cholos, or mestizos, and Indians who actually do the work of digging the wealth out of the mountains are a tough and often violent breed, courageous and at the same time superstitious. Their working lives are monotonous and constantly filled with danger. Toiling at great depths, they must sometimes be sprayed with water so they can withstand the extremely high temperatures. They constantly chew leaves of the coca plant for their narcotic effect, to deaden the strain of work and perhaps ease their fears, for they never know when a tunnel may cave in or a stick of dynamite accidentally come tumbling down a shaft to explode and kill everyone nearby. Outwardly, they show no fear and handle their dynamite with an air of disdain. If one inquires about a man with a missing arm or leg, the answer is often a shrug of the shoulders and the simple explanation, *"Dinamita."* Yet they are ever conscious of the perils they must face daily.

The presence of a woman in a mine is a sure sign of bad luck, and many miners believe their fate is really in the hands of a devil spirit, whom they call *Tío,* or Uncle. The Tío, they believe, is the real owner of the mine, and they must be careful not to offend him lest he take his revenge. To keep on his good side, they make images of him, in whatever shape their fancy takes, which they set in niches cut into the walls of the mine passages. The bodies are formed from ore, but heads, tails, eyes, and horns are made from a variety of objects such as nails, broken glass, and burnt-out light bulbs from the lamps they use in their helmets. When taking a drink, the miner is always careful to scatter a few drops on the ground to please the earth goddess, Pacha Mama.

Sometimes sacrifices of living animals are a part of the ritualistic appeasement of the devil *Huari* or other spiritual beings. These ceremonies, conducted by witch doctors or shamans called *yatiris,* are usually held deep in the earth at the site where some miner met his death, and the sacrificial victims are often young llamas. The pretty little animals may be loved by the miners, but the fact that they are chosen for sacrifice shows how much the Indians and cholos respect the powerful spirit.

Aboveground, a miner is quick to explode in a frenzy of excitement, probably as a release from the tensions under which he labors deep in the mines. Arguments easily turn into fights, in which sticks of dynamite are frequently the weapons. At the first sign of trouble at the mines—a rumor of layoffs or salary cuts, for example—the miners may seize the nearest official, and sometimes perfectly innocent foreign visitors have suddenly found themselves hostages to the miners' demands. To some extent, in fact, entire governments often find themselves at the mercy of the miners, who with dynamite in their hands turn into a sort of soldiery. In the 1952 revolution that brought Victor Paz Estenssoro into power, the miners from Oruro led by the fiery Juan Lechin marched into La Paz proudly wearing their helmets almost as a uniform.

Perhaps this spirit of unruliness and restlessness accounts for the fact that Carnival, the pre-Lenten holiday season celebrated throughout Bolivia, is at its gaudiest and liveliest in Oruro. Groups spend weeks organizing their presentations, preparing their brilliant costumes, and rehearsing their dances in secrecy. The best-known and most colorful is the *Diablada*, the Devil Dance, probably the most elaborate spectacle in Bolivian folklore. Miners in groups of one hundred or more wear huge grinning masks made of papier-mâché and painted in blinding colors, and they prance around with heavy, purposeful steps. In this dance, they are taking the role of the Devil, who is actually beseeching the *Virgen del Socavón,* or Virgin of the Mineshaft, in his own behalf. The origins of this dance date back to twelfth-century Spain, but in Bolivia it has taken on special significance related to mining.

There are other dances with strange and startling effects: the *Morenada,* deriving from the black slavery practiced on a relatively small scale in colonial days, in which participants with huge black masks shake noisemakers suggesting the rattling sounds of slaves' chains; the dance of *Los Incas,* portraying the clash between Inca and Spanish cultures; and the *Wacas,* a group of dances of Indian origin which burlesque the bullfights of the conquistadores or represent planting or other rites of agriculture.

Dancers lavishly costumed for *La Morenada.*

During the Carnival season, Oruro's few and small hotels are filled to overflowing. Families and groups of people also come by car or bus from La Paz to spend a day watching and participating in the fun. Well-off paceños, however, can take in the proceedings right in their living rooms—for television has come to the altiplano!

# 7

## The Altiplano and Lake Titicaca

Millions and millions of years ago, the space between the two great arms of the Andean mountain chain was a deep cleft. But as glaciers gouged their way down the high slopes like bulldozers, shoving rock and earth ahead of them, the cleft began to fill up. Streams born from melting snows brought down more material, and winds added their bit. Gradually the soil built up, layer after layer, to a depth of three thousand feet or more, turning the cleft into a vast tableland, or *meseta,* called the altiplano in Bolivia and the puna in Peru.

The altiplano is one of the world's great geographical wonders—a treeless tundra sitting high above the levels at which all other such plains occur. Occupying an oval formed by the Western Cordillera and the Cordillera Real, or Royal Cordillera, on the east, it measures some 520 miles from north to south, and averages 80 to 100 miles wide. Just about four-fifths of it lies in Bolivia. The bleak and barren landscape is painted in dull tones—browns and ochers and grays. It is practically devoid of greens, except when the rains fall between December and February. Then wild flowers bloom and puddles form everywhere to reflect the blue of the sky. But the water seeps quickly away, leaving little moisture to nourish plants during the arid winters.

Setting out from El Alto, perched on the rim of the La Paz canyon, to traverse the altiplano is a bit like crossing an ocean. The land seems to stretch on endlessly, smooth and flat in some places and rising in billows in others. You ride over a crest, and your vision is suddenly lengthened by miles. There in the distance the sun glints off the tin roofs of a group of low buildings, huddled together like a convoy of ships. Farther off, the horizon is broken by the jagged outlines of the snow-covered *cumbres,* or peaks, of the cordilleras.

In summer, sudden showers fall in a dozen places at once. Empty watercourses become flashing streams, forcing trucks and buses and cars to wait until the water recedes enough for them to waddle across the shallow fords. It is seldom worthwhile to build bridges; the streams die quickly soon after the rain stops. In the sere winters, the beds are dry, and all the landscape is parched. Plumes of dust mark the passage of vehicles along dirt roads far off in the distance.

Now the light is brilliant, in part because sunlight is reflected from the snows carpeting the faraway peaks. With the scarcity of moisture in the air, there is no haze. Distant objects can be seen so clearly and distinctly they appear to be close at hand. One can sunburn easily, yet shiver under thick blankets at night.

Vegetation is sparse, rarely growing higher than a foot or two. One plant seen everywhere in clumps is the *ichu* grass, or *paja brava* as the Spaniards called it. Too coarse and stiff to be eaten by any animal but the llamas and alpacas, those relatives of the camel, it is used by the campesino Indians to thatch the roofs of their tiny houses. However, donkeys and cows manage to find slim forage to munch on, and the altiplano supports sheep in great numbers. Flocks graze slowly, noses to the ground, usually tended by an Aymara Indian woman in her brown derby hat. Whether sitting or walking, she is always spinning. One hand is constantly twisting a foot-long spindle as the other alternately feeds it hanks of wool and pulls back on the fibers to thin them out. When sitting cross-legged, she places the sheep, llama, or alpaca wool in a bowl held between her knees in the valley formed by her several skirts. When moving about, she plucks the wool from a bunch tucked under an arm.

A feeling of loneliness and drabness pervades the altiplano, which may account for the Indian women's preference for bright-colored skirts and shawls. There are a few scattered towns, miles apart, but most of the people live in tiny hamlets,

Aymara woman of the altiplano spins alpaca fleece into yarn.

often merely a collection of adobe and stone huts. Windows
are simply square holes in the walls, without glass or any other
covering to keep out the wind. Nearby are walled enclosures
also made of adobe where animals can be penned up at night.
There is usually a beehive oven in the backyard, and occasionally a bicycle leans against an outside wall. Sometimes a
white flag flaps from a pole in front. It is a sign that the house-
holder is offering a homemade beer called *chicha*, which the
Indians are permitted to brew and sell among themselves.
Yellowish in color, it is made from corn or other grain. To
start the process of fermentation, women chew kernels and
spit out the saliva into bowls.

Inside the houses, there is seldom any furniture but a
woven basket or two for storage. People sit right on the
earthen floor, or on llama or alpaca hides laid over mounds of
ichu grass. They eat from bowls and pans, using their fingers
instead of forks or spoons. On the walls hang the Aymara
woman's collection of handmade derby hats, a form of personal wealth like jewelry in other societies. When a woman can
afford a factory-manufactured article, her first choice is
usually a sewing machine. However, other products of the industrial age are beginning to appear. Some of the boys and
men have bicycles, and it is common to see a rider steering
one with one hand while the other holds a transistor radio to
his ear.

Potatoes and cereals are the staple diet on the altiplano, sup-
plemented from time to time with eggs, poultry, mutton,
cheeses made from llama milk, and even llama meat itself.
The potatoes are usually eaten in a dehydrated form called
*chuno,* and preparing them is quite a job. After a long soaking
in water, they are left out in the open for several weeks. Alter-
nate heating by the sun and chilling at night drives out most

In making *chuno*, the farmer stamps all the water out of the potatoes.

of the moisture, and the campesinos squeeze out the rest by treading on the pulpy mass with their feet. The final product has a nutlike flavor and consistency. Dehydrated *oca*, another tuber native to the altiplano, is prepared in the same manner.

Barley is about the only imported grain crop that does well in the altiplano. The climate is too cold for corn, which grows plentifully at lower altitudes in the high valleys, but there are several native grains, including quinoa and canahui, that are used to make a nutritive but rather tasteless porridge called *ppesche*. The red-tufted quinoa and the bright green patches of barley, often growing some distance away from the nearest house, are a welcome change from the dreary hues of the thin brush and grasses.

The slopes of the low hills are often a checkerboard of tiny plots outlined by walls of stones. But for all the boulders removed, the spaces enclosed seem just as stony. Many of the walls are the remains of terraces built in the days of the Incas but since abandoned.

To work their plots, the campesinos have only a few simple tools—a stick with a pointed stone tied on one end to open holes in the ground, and occasionally a simple homemade wooden plow. The plows are shoved or pulled by the campesinos themselves, for animals of traction such as bullocks are seldom used on the altiplano. And no one could possibly afford a tractor.

Everywhere in the altiplano there are ferias, open-air markets or fairs where people exchange what they make or grow, as well as the latest bits of news. The busiest, of course, are those held in the towns, but even far from villages an empty roadside field will serve as the site for a feria. Articles to be traded or sold are simply laid out on the ground, sometimes under a floppy canopy of cloth tied to poles. Buyers are so few and the produce so pitifully simple that it all seems hardly worthwhile. Yet people will spend a whole day there. For persons living in the solitudes of the altiplano, a feria is as much a social gathering as it is a commercial affair.

A typical feria is the one held in the town of Tiahuanaco, halfway between the archeological ruins with the same name and the tiny port of Guaqui on Lake Titicaca. People begin to gather early in the day in the square in front of the unpainted adobe-brick church. Some arrive by truck, and others in buses with their roofs piled high with boxes and bundles, and frequently a bicycle strapped onto the back end. Women in their bowler hats, their babies riding on their backs in awayo shawls, stroll among the little heaps of potatoes and oca, puny fruit, eggs, and coca leaves, or the shawls and ponchos and pots and pans hanging from rickety frames made of poles. From a loudspeaker over the church door comes recorded organ music, or the voice of the priest delivering a sermon. A girl of fifteen or sixteen in her white bridal gown and veil slips through the entrance for her wedding. The men gather in little groups to gossip, or frequent the *peluquerías* to have their hair cut or the bars for a drink of chicha, where they are careful first to spill a few drops on the floor to honor the earth goddess Pacha Mama.

On one side of the plaza, the men and boys who make up a brass band, all dressed in their well-worn black suits, are holding an impromptu rehearsal before boarding a bus that will

A wedding party leaving a church.

take them to La Paz for a folklore festival. Among their instruments, tubas seem to predominate. A curious reason is often given for the popularity of the tuba in Bolivia. A school principal who wanted to organize a band wrote an English merchant asking for the instruments he would need. Since the merchant was overstocked on tubas, he used them to fill most of the order. But whether he produces it from imported tubas and trombones, from homemade wooden flutes such as the *quena,* the *pinquillo,* the *tarka,* or a set of pipes called the *zampoña,* or from the five-string guitar, the charango, music is important to the dweller on the altiplano with its wearisome loneliness and isolation.

Yet for all its apparent sameness, the altiplano and its environs abound in unusual and varied sights. At Visachani, an hour's drive south of El Alto on the highway to Oruro, fossilized impressions of trilobites, shrimplike creatures that became extinct hundreds of millions of years ago, can be picked up by the dozens. Comanche, fifty miles from La Paz, is famous for its century plants. A member of the bromeliad family and hence a relative of the pineapple, this strange plant grows ten to fifteen feet tall, and botanists say it requires about one hundred years before it is ready to bloom. There are iciclelike formations of eroded rock and soil at Achocalla, lovely orchards and orange-colored hills near Luribay, and at Urmiri hot springs come gushing out of the ground. Gloomy caves lie at the foot of Mount Illampu near the town of Sorata, and up on the slopes of Chacaltaya, where the United Nations maintains a cosmic ray laboratory near the world's highest ski run, there are incredible views of peaks and the altiplano.

Nothing on the altiplano, however, is more impressive than Lake Titicaca, the highest navigable body of water in the world and the mythical birthplace of the first Inca rulers. Lying half in Peru and half in Bolivia, its intense blue waters cover an area more than twice the size of Utah's Great Salt Lake. In some places, such as the region around Guaqui where a long channel had to be dredged to allow ships to dock, the low-lying shore is flat and swampy. In other places, rocky precipices plunge abruptly to the water's edge. Here birdlife is plentiful—gulls, ducks, plover, and avocet with their upward curving beaks. Indian fishermen bring in, among other fish, salmon trout introduced to the lake from North America as an important part of their catch.

Besides the steamers that ply overnight between Guaqui and the Peruvian port of Puno, hydrofoils skim over the surface carrying passengers from the mainland to Jaguar Rock, or the Isle of the Sun, and to towns such as Hutajata and Copacabana. The latter is a charming place, with groves of eucalyptus giving permanent green to the landscape. The land sloping to the shore is covered with walled cultivated plots that from the distance look like a patchwork quilt or a tiled floor. The town lies on a peninsula that would cut the lake in two were it not for the narrow Strait of Tiquina, and it is famous for its shrine of the Virgin of Copacabana, or the Black Madonna. Many years ago, a replica of the statue of the Virgin was presented to the people of Rio de Janeiro in Brazil, where it was installed in a church on a beach, now the famous Beach of Copacabana.

In the shallow parts of Lake Titicaca, a useful reed called the *totora* grows plentifully. Boats, or rafts, made of totora reeds and called *balsas,* at one time were the only craft available to the Titicaca fishermen. Built to look something like a hammock with a high narrow bow and stern, the balsas last about a year before they become too waterlogged to paddle or sail and must be dragged up on the shore to dry out. Although many

Aymara fishermen of Lake Titicaca use boats made from totora reeds.

fishermen now use wooden rowboats, the picturesque totora balsa is still part of the Titicaca setting.

Strangely enough, the totora reed of antiquity is linked to a modern scientific experiment. After his epic journey across the Pacific in his raft *Kon-Tiki,* the explorer Thor Heyerdahl became convinced that expeditions from Egypt more than two thousand years ago had probably managed to cross the Atlantic in large rafts made of papyrus, a reed similar to the totora found in the Nile River Valley. To prove that such a voyage was possible, he had such a raft made, which he called the *Ra,* and set forth in it. This first attempt was a failure, however, which Heyerdahl attributed to the raft's having been improperly constructed. For a second try, he had four Lake Titicaca fishermen from the Bolivian village of Suriki brought all the way to Safi in Morocco, where they set to work building a new raft. In less than two months, the Aymara fishermen had completed the craft named *Ra II,* a huge reproduction of the tiny balsas they had often made at home, although they found the stiff papyrus reed much harder to work with than the more pliable totora. In the summer of 1972, the *Ra II* brought Dr. Heyerdahl and his fellow adventurers, drifting and sailing, safely across the Atlantic Ocean to the Caribbean island of Barbados.

Because the temperature of its waters remains at a constant fifty-five degrees Fahrenheit, Lake Titicaca has a modifying effect on the climate of the surrounding area, making it milder than other altiplano regions during the winter. The waters retain heat of the sun because of their great depth, measured in one place at 986 feet. However, no one knows how deep the deepest parts really are. Another mystery is what happens to all the water that enters the lake. Over the years, the water level has dropped, although the amount entering the lake from snow-fed streams is more than that lost through evaporation or runoff. Some water probably just seeps down through the bottom, perhaps to emerge as underground streams someplace on the outside slopes of the cordilleras. In addition, part drains out through the lake's only surface outlet, the Desaguadero River, a shallow stream that meanders two hundred miles southward into Lake Poopó, shallow and much smaller than Titicaca, and extremely salty. Around Poopó are large deposits of salt, covering huge areas called *salares* where absolutely nothing will grow. Lake Poopó drains through a sluggish stream called the Lakajahuira, which after three or four miles simply disappears into the earth.

The remnants of two dwindling Indian peoples live in the region of southern Titicaca and Poopó, quite different from both the Aymaras who dominate the altiplano and the Bolivian Quechuas who live mostly in the high valleys and the yungas, the narrow gorges that plunge from the altiplano down to the jungles of the Oriente. These small tribes are the Uros and the Chipayas. The former are primitive folk living mostly on fish from Titicaca and speaking no other tongue but their own. The Chipayas, too, once lived near Titicaca, but more powerful peoples, probably the Aymaras, pushed them gradually south onto the arid salt fields around Lake Poopó. For the Chipayas, almost everything they can see or touch is the dwelling of a spirit—rocks, mountains, a stick left in a doorway, animals, even a church tower. They build altars out of earth and stone, leaving a hole for the resident spirit to enter and leave, and they claim to be descended from *chullpas,* which are square burial towers left everywhere by the mysterious pre-Inca people of the Tiahuanaco civilization. In addition to their own language, called Puquina, the Chipayas speak Aymara.

Forbidding, inhospitable as it is, the altiplano exercises a strange fascination over people born upon it, or who get to know it well. Bolivia's government has been encouraging campesinos to move from the highlands to the fertile lowlands of the Oriente, where life is less harsh. Among the Quechuas, the resettlement program has had some success. But the Aymara's heart belongs to his altiplano homeland, and when he leaves it for any purpose he longs to return.

Through their stay abroad, for example, the Aymara fisher-

Street in the altiplano town of Copacabana.

men who built the *Ra II* for Thor Heyerdahl saw many things that were new and wondrous to them: airplanes, tall buildings, hotel rooms with shower baths, even the ocean itself. Yet they seemed to take everything in stride, seldom showing the least sign of surprise at the newest marvel. Forced to surrender their supplies of chuno to foreign customs and health officials, they ate the local food without complaint, but without enthusiasm either. Whenever they felt homesick, they were comforted by touching the little white stones from the shores of Titicaca given them on their departure by their wives and other relatives.

# 8

## The Yungas and the High Valleys

East of the Andes Mountains, on the opposite side of the Royal Cordillera from the altiplano, lies the rest of Bolivia, divided into two geographical regions. One is the savanna and forest flatlands of the Oriente, spreading out from the very feet of the mountains. The other part consists of the flanks of the mountains themselves. This is an intermediate zone between the highlands and the lowlands. Accounting for about a tenth of Bolivia's total area, it supports a third of the country's five million people.

In the north, this zone is narrow. The land drops away abruptly through the yungas, gorges and steep valleys that plunge almost vertically to the matted jungle floor skirting the Beni River and its tributaries. Farther south, this in-between area broadens into parallel ridges and spurs, with gently sloping valleys in some places that seem to have been partially filled up. Actually, these valles, or valleys, are wide basins, at altitudes from six thousand to nine thousand feet, where the climate is one of eternal spring. Here agriculture flourishes, and settlements are numerous.

The high valleys and flanks of the intermediate zone are well watered. In this part of South America, the prevailing

Spectacular highway from La Paz to the yungas drops sharply from snow-covered slopes.

winds blow from east to west. They sweep across two thousand miles of plains and swamplands picking up moisture. When the air meets the barrier of the Andes, it rises, and the moisture is released to fall as rain on the eastern slopes. That is why the altiplano and everything west of it is generally so dry.

A ride down through the yungas is one of the most spectacular and hair-raising journeys anywhere on earth. It is easy enough at first, on the road out of La Paz heading toward Unduavi. For half an hour or so the road winds upward, crossing the line marking the beginning of perpetual snow, until it reaches La Cumbre, the summit, at 15,250 feet. Then the drop begins. Often chiseled into the very walls of gorges, the road twists downward, swinging around blind curves that leave one staring straight out over the edge of a precipice. Cloud wreaths float upward like rising steam, and in places the road ducks under waterfalls.

At Unduavi, the highway divides, but for thrills and scenic marvels there is little to choose between the two forks. Gradually the landscape changes. The dun-colored world of the altiplano seems far behind, on some other planet, and one is in the midst of green again, in warm, soft air heavy with the scent of vegetation. Jungle growth becomes thick—ten-foot-high tree ferns, vines called *llianas* as thick as a man's arm, hardwood trees of a dozen varieties used in making beautiful furniture.

Roads in the yungas are unpaved, yet precisely because they traverse such dangerous terrain, the government tends to take special care with their maintenance, and they are really among Bolivia's best. Trucks account for most of the traffic. They are flatbed types, fitted with canvas coverings, and they are just as often filled with people as with produce, since they are the cheapest form of travel in the area. Drivers must be extremely cautious, for a curve misjudged by a foot or two can mean plunging over a sheer drop of a thousand feet or more. Crudely made crosses painted white mark the sites of just such disasters and are visited periodically by bereaved families, who leave flowers and lighted candles to honor the memory of the victims.

Coming up, trucks haul logs from the jungle; produce such as pineapples, bananas, papayas, oranges, cotton, coffee; all sorts of vegetables; and great bundles of coca leaves which are consumed in large quantities on the altiplano. The trucks often return empty, but the most frequent cargoes are kerosine, cloth, beer and canned food, miners' tools—and miners themselves. The streams flowing out of the yungas are panned for gold, and around the town of Tipuani a regular gold rush is on. In the Quechua tongue, *cor* is the word for gold, and it appears over and over again throughout Bolivia in place names such as Coroico and Coripata, both situated in the yungas.

To lower transportation costs and promote faster development of the semitropical yungas, as well as to provide a more direct access to the jungles of the Beni and Pando departments and the unexploited wealth they contain, governments have often thought of building better highway connections and even a railway from La Paz. In fact, one attempt at a railroad was actually made, but the line got no farther than La Cumbre. Although the cost of bridging or tunneling through dozens of gorges would be immense, the idea of a railroad into the yungas has not been entirely abandoned.

The descent into the high valleys farther south is easier, although, in its way, the scenery is no less spectacular than the misty yungas. In the mild climate of these broad, almost flat valleys, wheat, corn, temperate-zone fruit and other crops that will not grow in the altiplano thrive in abundance. Three of the high valleys are important centers of settlement. Their names derive from the dominant city in each. They are Tarija, farthest from La Paz and close to the Argentine border, almost on the edge of the sandy, semiarid part of the Chaco; Sucre, Bolivia's official capital, aristocratic, practically a museum in itself; and Cochabamba, the second largest city in the country and by far the most important of the three. These cities and the valleys they lie in live principally by supplying food to La Paz and the mining towns of the altiplano. The Cochabamba Valley, for example, is still often called "the breadbasket" of Bolivia, although industry in and around the city is gaining momentum.

The quickest way to get to Cochabamba, of course, is to fly, and the flight path from La Paz takes you practically across the white face of towering Mount Illimani. An hour later when you step off the plane, among the first things to strike your attention is the array of gorgeous roses in front of the airport terminal, a harbinger of the bright flowers to be found everywhere in this city of eternal spring.

However, air travelers miss the chance of seeing and savoring close up the varied Bolivian landscape that only a journey by land provides. A trip by railroad, on the ferrobus, takes thirteen hours, and the descent into Cochabamba Valley is so steep in places that the tracks can be seen tracing their way back and forth at five different levels below. Another route is the nine-hour drive on the highway over the corrugated back of the cordilleras. After leaving La Paz, the road skirts to the left of Oruro and soon runs out of pavement. From there on, it dips and climbs from ridge to ridge over treeless moorland, with faint green cultivated patches that look as though they would slide off if the slopes were canted another notch higher. The road crosses and recrosses the pipeline through which oil is pumped from the eastern fields of Camiri to La Paz or to

Arica on the Pacific coast. Every so often there are special stations on the "down" side to let off the tremendous pressure that otherwise would burst the pipes.

It is a lonely journey. Traffic is sparse, mostly trucks and rickety buses. There are few villages to pass, all without restaurants or even service stations for gasoline. Drivers refill their tanks from demijohns stored at truckers' stops. Flocks of stately llamas and alpacas graze on the slopes, and the young boys watching over them come running to meet passing vehicles, waving the floppy felt hats they wear over their knitted wool lluchos. Dogs crouch along the highway. Their noses come up at the sound of an approaching vehicle, and they rise on their haunches to follow it with their eyes in hope that someone will toss them a tidbit of food. The bus or truck passes, and the dogs slump down again to resume their watch.

Finally the road runs along the rims of deep valleys and gulches, with walls of yellow, brown, red, and gray, and then begins the steep descent into the broad, well-watered basin of the Cochabamba Valley. Far below in the blue haze are checkered planted areas, generally edged with darker lines of casuarina pines or feathery eucalyptus.

The city of Cochabamba itself, with its population of 150,000, snuggles against the slopes of the Andes, gentle here and broken by gullies edged with stream-borne bits of rock and earth. Tunari, the highest peak visible from the city, looms in the background.

Cochabamba is a pleasant city of squares and plazas. Except for a few high-rise structures in the center of town, the old Spanish-style buildings predominate, their once reddish tile roofs now weathered gray and almost black. Some roofs are pagoda shaped where they change angles to extend out over the sidewalks. Narrow streets are all at right angles, and there are few stoplights. Whichever approaching driver honks his horn first has the right of way. From the outside, many of the low buildings hugging the sidewalks look uninteresting—a blank wall with a wooden or iron-grille doorway in the middle. But inside is a charming private world, with connected dwellings opening onto one or more quiet patios awash in bougainvillea, poinsettias, and other flowering shrubs. The streets are kept clean by squads of Indian women in white stovepipe hats, typical of Quechuas in this region, who sweep them with brooms made of bundles of twigs.

Avenida Ballivian begins at the Plaza Colón (Columbus Square), with its banks of flowers and stone-arched bridge over a quiet pool. It is at the edge of the city's older but still fashionable residential district. On Sundays, well-dressed families stroll beneath stately palms and tall, shady eucalyptus and pines. The late afternoons and evenings are cool, and the younger people wear capes or sweaters of fine alpaca wool with blending colors designed into Indian motifs. Here the showplace residences are more open to view. Set in spacious plots surrounded by well-tended gardens (geraniums planted next to walls grow six feet high), they all seem to have been built in the 1930s and 40s, although they are immaculately kept up. Most are surrounded by iron-grille fences and sometimes walls with shards of glass cemented into the top to keep out prowlers. Farther out, across the muddy Rocha River, is a newer residential section, where the houses cling to the slopes leading up to the Andean backdrop. Here, too, is an unusual restaurant that provides a pleasant atmosphere for lunch. It has a small terraced garden crammed with chrysanthemums, roses, gladioli, asters, and dozens of other showy flowers, as well as citrus trees hanging with oranges, grapefruit as big as footballs, and cages with chattering birds from all parts of the country. The specialty meal is wild duckling prepared with shrimp flown in from the coastal area of Chile.

Cochabamba's commercial district centers around the main square, the Fourteenth of September Plaza. Here many of the buildings extend out over the sidewalks on colonnades. Everywhere there are *librerías,* bookstores, for Cochabamba ranks with La Paz as a literary and publishing center. All the buildings on the square, including the large town hall of stucco, once were white but were repainted pink on the order of the *alcalde,* or mayor, in honor of a visit by President Tito of "Red" Yugoslavia. Many elderly heads of state and other dignitaries who visit Bolivia often skip La Paz because of the rigors of the altitude, and are received instead with official formalities in Cochabamba. On such occasions, Bolivia's state dinner service and other symbols of government are shipped down from La Paz by train, to be returned after the visit is over. Besides Yugoslavia's Marshal Tito, French president Charles de Gaulle was another foreign head of state for whom honors were rendered in Cochabamba.

Certainly visitors feel easier at the lower altitude of Cochabamba, although at 8,430 feet it is still more than a mile high. And getting around its level streets is a pleasant change from the exhausting climbs and descents in La Paz. There are many interesting places to visit. At the University of San Simón, with a campus in contrast to La Paz' San Andrés "skyscraper" university, is an archeological museum where the history of Bolivia's early peoples can be traced in pottery and carvings, weapons and tools. Some of the objects come from a burial site of Cayacayani in the Santiváñez Valley twenty-five miles southwest of Cochabamba, and the ruins of the vast Inca fortress at Incallacta, at a lower altitude in the direction of Santa Cruz. This fortress was built around 1370 and rebuilt in

1425 after its destruction during a revolt by local tribes against the Inca power. Later it was raided by lowland Indians from Paraguay, led by Portuguese adventurers. The Inca Huáscar, brother of the ill-fated Atahualpa, sent a force led by two of his best generals to wipe out the raiders and repair the damage they left.

A visit to La Coronilla, a hill on the edge of the city, affords splendid vistas of the broad Cochabamba Valley and its rim of surrounding mountains. Here, too, is a historical landmark, a statue honoring the women of Cochabamba who fought with sticks and clubs against the Spanish colonial soldiers who had imprisoned most of the town's young men during a revolutionary movement. La Coronilla also serves as a huge outdoor meeting place for political rallies and itinerant preachers, like the young and handsome "miracle-worker" known as Ruibal, who on one Sunday drew a crowd of fifty thousand to hear his sermon.

Every Wednesday and Saturday, a feria is held at La Cancha, near the newer of Cochabamba's two railroad stations. Besides the fruits and vegetables, the articles of clothing and the pots and pans offered at ferias throughout Bolivia, there are mounds of sandals fashioned out of the treads of truck tires, musical instruments such as the charango, made from armadillo shells, and all sorts of other handcraft items. Men thread their way among the stalls staggering under the weight of huge plaited baskets filled with potatoes or fat ears of corn. Shelled corn is spread out in semicircles around a squatting Quechua woman in her tall white hat, who carefully arranges and rearranges the various-colored kernels into intricate patterns of yellows, whites, grays, and reds. Dozens of varieties of corn are grown in the Cochabamba Valley, with big bulging ears that are almost all kernel and very little cob.

The simple, elementary merchandise bought and sold at the La Cancha fair is in striking contrast with the riches and luxury encountered at another Cochabamba landmark, the Palácio de Portales, the town house built by the tin magnate Simón Patiño. Marble floors and alabaster statuary, rich tapestries imported from Europe along with European architects and decorators, carved mahogany staircases and glittering chandeliers, all testify to the immense wealth of the simple miner who rose to become one of the richest men on earth. Outside the city of Pairumani is another Patiño creation, a vast estate named Villa Albina, in honor of Patiño's wife. Here, too, are marble statues and formal gardens, a family mausoleum, and in front of the mansion a huge rock taken from the rich tin vein originally found by Patiño.

The road to Villa Albina passes a stone's throw from Vinto, a stop on the railroad to Oruro. Here campesinos come to lay out their produce along the tracks for buyers who come down from the mines. Potatoes, carrots, onions, beets, cabbages, and corn are piled into heaps, and there are tiny tomatoes and fruit such as avocados, figs, and a rather puny type of peach.

A number of suburban towns are growing up around Cochabamba, from which workers commute to jobs in the city in small buses and trucks. One of the largest is Quillacolla, about a dozen miles from Cochabamba. Buses draw up around the main square, with its shabby little stores, one of which is the workshop that makes and repairs the white stovepipe hats of which the Quechua women are so fond. The hats appear to be made out of paper or straw, but are actually tightly crocheted thread. The fabric is then starched, blocked, and finally painted with white lead. The manner in which the black ribbon is looped and tied around the base of the crown tells whether the wearer is single or married or a widow looking

Women conduct the trade in the Indian marketplace.

for another husband. Quechua women of the Cochabamba area are proud of these hats, which they wear at various angles. Usually they refuse to pose in them for photographs, and anyone caught trying to snap a picture on the sly becomes the object of resentful stares. However, the hatmakers themselves are quite willing to sell their output to any buyer with the price.

The pace of life for the *cochabambinos,* as the residents of the valley are called, is unhurried. Families with small country places called *fincas* invite one another to spend weekends there. When friends get together the conversation often turns to politics. The Cochabamba region has produced a number of Bolivian presidents, including the infamous Melgarejo and the popular René Barrientos. For young people of well-to-do families social life is apt to center around clubs rather than schools. Among sports, soccer is by far the favorite, but tennis and volleyball are played and swimming is popular. Cochabamba basketball teams have been winning national championships for years.

Cochabamba is a hardworking city, but a quiet one also. It goes to bed early, and wakes up early too, to the ringing of church bells. Despite its size it has a small-town atmosphere. In many ways, the visitor gets the feeling that the city enjoyed a spurt of growth a couple of decades ago, which then ran out of gas. Older residents say that the 1952 land reform was to blame by halting the income from estates that were split up and awarded to the campesinos. However, new industries are beginning to sprout. There are plants processing dairy products, a tire factory, textile mills, ceramic factories, breweries, and an oil refinery that is bringing some small chemical plants in its wake. Cochabamba seems to be entering a new era of growth.

Sucre, on the other hand, is a city where nothing seems to change. Founded in 1538, about one hundred years before the Puritans were forming townships around Massachusetts Bay, the city was progressively called Charcas, La Plata, and Chuquisaca before it was renamed Sucre in honor of Bolivia's first president. Although it appears on maps as Bolivia's official capital, of the three main branches of government only the Supreme Court is located there, with the executive and congress functioning in La Paz. Today Sucre is a quiet backwater of colonial charm, its architectural treasures from the past remaining virtually intact to this very day.

From Cochabamba, flights of the national airline Lloyd Aereo Boliviano depart for Sucre every other day, and the trip by air takes only an hour. One can also go by road, starting out on the paved highway heading east through the Punata Valley but turning right onto an unpaved road about halfway before reaching Santa Cruz. From the turnoff, the road coils back up over the mountains, skirting the sandy region of cactus and scrubby vegetation that extends up from the Chaco. Finally the highway winds down into the Chuquisaca Valley and on to Sucre. A longer and even more roundabout route that takes two full days is to return from Cochabamba over the cordillera to Oruro. From there one can continue by highway or railway through Potosí and on through wild and fantastic scenery to Sucre. But because road conditions are hazardous, a trip from Oruro by train is probably preferable. If one goes by highway, caravans of llamas are frequently seen, some of them bearing salt from the Uyuni flats on the altiplano down into the high valleys.

Sucre is an aristocratic city and an intellectual center, and the people are proud of its past and their heritage. It has many fine homes, required by law to be whitewashed every two years. Many have the overhanging fretwork balconies typical of early Spanish colonial architecture. They were built with wealth accumulated from *haciendas,* large plantations or farms, from the earliest times when the city was the seat of the Audiencia of Charcas, subject to the Viceroyalty of Lima and for a time the Viceroyalty of La Plata headquartered in Buenos Aires.

The chuquisaqueños, as the people of Sucre and the Department of Chuquisaca are called, give great importance to the role their ancestors played in Bolivia's earliest struggles for independence. Sucre's University of San Francisco Xavier was one of the centers of liberal ideas that gave rise to the movement for separation from Spain, and like Cochabamba the city is the birthplace of many of the nation's presidents. Artists and writers and other intellectual leaders also found life in Sucre and the surrounding countryside stimulating to their imagination. Preeminent among them was Franz Tamayo, Bolivia's best-known literary figure and one of the earliest to pay homage to the cultural contributions of Bolivia's native peoples, which the Creoles tended to overlook and even hide. Tamayo's own mother, of whom he was intensely proud, was a full-blooded Indian. She was always present at parties and gatherings held in his Sucre home, when he read from his works or played the piano for his guests. Before leaving, it is said, they were expected to make token purchases of potatoes and other produce raised on his farm.

Bolivia's National Library is in Sucre, housed in a building on Calle España (Spain Street). It contains the nation's most important archives, as well as such treasured volumes as a first edition of Dr. Samuel Johnson's famous dictionary of the English language. There is also a special museum called the Casa de la Libertad, the House of Liberty, where documents and artifacts relating to Bolivia's independence from Spain are preserved, in the same way that Independence Hall in Philadelphia, with the original of the United States Constitution and the Liberty Bell, is a shrine to the American Revolution. An immense bust of Simón Bolívar, twice the height of a man and carved in wood by the Bolivian sculptor Mauro Nunez, sits brooding in one of the quiet rooms.

Sucre is a grove of churches. They seem to have sprung up at every corner and are far more noticeable than churches in places like La Paz where their towers are overshadowed by skyscrapers. Many of them have the simpler, more austere lines of churches built before the more flamboyant and embellished baroque style came into fashion. Sucre's cathedral has an unusual bell tower—and an unusual number of bells—with saints and angels and other ceramic figures poised on the rising set of corners. La Recoleta, a monastery and school built in 1601, stands on a bit of high ground overlooking the city and the valley. Its four gracious cloisters are bright with flowers and heavy with the scent of orange blossoms, and one contains a cedar tree reputed to be hundreds of years old, a

One of the many churches in Sucre, Bolivia's official capital.

withering remnant of the region's cedar forests that were cut down for building timbers. For a brief period following Bolivia's independence, La Recoleta served as a barracks and prison, and a plaque on the way upstairs to the choir marks the site where President Pedro Blanco was executed, just two days after he took office.

Just outside of Sucre is one of the most curious buildings to be found anywhere. Now a military academy, it was once the residence of the wealthy Argandoña industrial family, who early in this century spent most of their time traveling about Europe developing a passion for European styles of architecture. Just about all of them—and a few from other cultures— are represented in the mansion called La Glorieta they built back home in Sucre. A Gothic belfry surmounts the chapel next to the main Florentine building, with its Moorish portico and Byzantine tower. Melding all this together must have been a nerve-racking job for the Italian architect, but somehow he managed to achieve a certain sense of harmony.

Past La Glorieta toward Potosí is the luxuriant Valley of Ñucchu, with large and well-kept haciendas used as weekend retreats by their wealthy chuquisaqueño owners. In another direction, southeast toward Tarija, is Tarabuco, and there one finds something quite different. The town is a Quechua Indian village, where virtually no Spanish is spoken. The Tarabuco men wear one of the strangest costumes encountered anywhere in Bolivia: felt hats shaped like the leather or metal helmets of the Spanish conquistadores, many decorated with spangles and sequins, and short ponchos of red and black horizontal stripes, with the red predominating.

Tarija, in the lowest of the three main "high valleys," is almost on the edge of the Chaco and fairly close to the border of Argentina. Like Sucre, it is a quiet town of Spanish-style homes with secluded inner patios. It is about three hours by air from La Paz, on a flight that makes a stopover in Sucre. Only persons hardened to train travel in Bolivia would try to reach Tarija from La Paz by rail. A ferrobus takes fifteen hours overnight to reach Villazón right on the Argentine border, and from there one must ride a bus for another six hours to get to Tarija.

The capital of the Department of Tarija, the city is really a small town (population thirty-six thousand). With its red terracotta roofs, tree-lined streets, and orchards and vineyards in the valley formed by the Guadalquivir River, the city and its surrounding area are reminiscent of Spain's province of Andalusia. The *chapacos,* or residents of Tarija, are fond of music and have developed several types of instruments all their own. Among them is the *erque,* a wind instrument made from a cow's horn, and the *caja,* a small drum that can be played with one hand. Most unusual, however is the *caña,* a ten-foot-long tube with a cow's horn at the end.

In life-style the chapaco is closer to Argentinians than to other Bolivians. Here the women carry large bundles on their heads instead of wrapped in shawls on their backs as the Quechua and Aymara women do. In fact, most of the people have light skin and there are many blond heads, indicating the complete absence of Indian ancestry.

In the rest of Bolivia, however, the chapaco is considered a sort of "hick," a person from the countryside. His easygoing ways and slower speech are often mimicked, especially in jokes about characters who are slow on the uptake.

# 9

## Santa Cruz—Signpost to the Future

Enamored of the mineral wealth of the Andes, the Bolivians of the highlands for years practically turned their backs on what is now emerging as their country's richest treasure trove. This is the Oriente, the East, a vast expanse of jungle and savanna flatlands spreading out from the foothills of the Andes to cover two-thirds of Bolivia's land area.

The change came about because the attitude of governments in La Paz in the past couple of decades has shifted from indifference and neglect to intense interest. As a result, the Oriente is in the midst of a boom, spewing out new wealth that for years lay untouched principally because of inaccessibility to markets. The subsoil is yielding oil, natural gas, and iron ore. Cotton, sugar, rice, tobacco, coffee, and other crops are being harvested from the surface. Hardwood is being cut from the forests. To be sure, these riches are coming mostly from Santa Cruz, the largest of Bolivia's nine departments, or states, accounting for over half the territory of the Oriente. But other areas to the north and northwest are beginning to develop in its wake.

The bustle, the fervor of eastern Bolivia can best be sensed in the city of Santa Cruz de la Sierra, Sacred Cross of the

Mountains, from which the Department of Santa Cruz takes its name. Almost in the middle of South America, the city has changed overnight from a sleepy frontier town, where horsemen from the plains tied their mounts to colonnades along the roofed-over sidewalks, into a thriving hub of commercial activity. The colonnades are still there, but the streets where only a few years ago squeaking oxcarts churned through mud in summer and stirred up dust in the dry season are paved with concrete blocks or asphalt. Autos, buses, and trucks imported mostly from Japan and next-door Brazil circulate through the narrow streets in the center and along the newly built concentric avenues that circle the city. Motorcycles rocket back and forth between the city and settlements springing up beyond its outskirts. Jeeps and heavy-duty trucks lumber across the sandy plains going south to the oil fields or on to Tarija or into Paraguay and Argentina, "making their own roads," as their drivers say. They assure you there are roads everywhere throughout the department, but only a couple of highways are paved and most turn out to be little more than a set of ruts. In fact, a majority of the city's taxis are Jeeps, so they can serve passengers who live on the unpaved roads outside of town.

Transportation was the main key to the revival of what is actually one of Bolivia's oldest cities, for Santa Cruz, the department's capital, was founded in 1561. Its founder was a Spanish captain, Ñuflo de Chavez, who came up the Pilcomayo River with a troop of soldiers and Guaraní Indians from Paraguay. Actually, the city he started was 120 miles east of the present site, to which it was moved because of its better location where the *llanos,* or savannas, meet the foothills of the sierra, twenty miles farther west. Colonization went on, and the struggling ranchers and planters found an outlet for their

Bullock carts are still used extensively in the province of Santa Cruz.

produce over narrow trails twisting into the high valleys and thence over the Cordillera Real to the altiplano.

Then came the age of railroad building in the highlands, and it almost dealt Santa Cruz a deathblow. The railroads were constructed to make it easier for Bolivia to export its minerals. But by the same token they made it more economical to import food and raw materials from abroad than to buy those carried by the slow mule and llama caravans that labored up through the passes from the Oriente. With their outside markets gone, the *cruceños,* or inhabitants of Santa Cruz, only bothered to raise what they could consume themselves, and the economy of the whole Oriente just about collapsed.

In fact, many cruceños were ready to give up on La Paz and considered breaking away from Bolivia to form their own country. They turned their eyes south and east to the markets of Argentina and Brazil, which both began poking railroads in the direction of Santa Cruz de la Sierra. The Argentines got there first, with an offshoot of the line that runs to Sucre. The Brazilians arrived quite a bit later, with a narrow-gauge affair that runs six hundred miles across the empty llanos from Puerto Suarez on the border opposite the Brazilian city of Corumbá.

In La Paz, meanwhile, instead of thinking of Santa Cruz as a troublesome province way to the east whose development could safely be left to the future, the government began looking at the entire Oriente for its potential wealth. A paved highway from Cochabamba to Santa Cruz de la Sierra was started in 1945 as part of the United States' program of aid to Latin America, and the project was probably the one with the greatest impact of all. For when the difficult job—described by some engineers as the most challenging bit of highway construction undertaken up to its time—was finished a decade later, the Bolivian Oriente started to come to life again with a rediscovered feeling of unity with the rest of Bolivia. Sugar and beef, cotton and rice, soybeans, lumber, and other products from the Santa Cruz area as well as being exported, chiefly to Argentina, could now be trucked swiftly to Cochabamba, and from there go by rail or highway up to the altiplano. Now it made sense for the government to foster colonization in the fertile Oriente with people from the parched altiplano and settlers from foreign countries too. The newcomers included Japanese and even a wandering group of German-descended people called Mennonites, members of a religious sect some of whose members settled in the United States.

The 315-mile Cochabamba–Santa Cruz highway crosses a variety of terrain. It goes through a misty valley with ghostlike trees, actually called Siberia, before dropping down into the warmer climes of tropical rain forests, sandy semidesert, and on to the hot and humid flatland around the city of Santa Cruz. Comfortable buses with reclining seats make the run in ten to twelve hours, depending on which direction they are heading. But there is no air conditioning, so passengers not interested in the scenery prefer to journey in the cool of night.

Travelers arriving by plane alight at a somewhat primitive airport, equipped nonetheless to handle smaller jets of the two- and three-engine type. They whoosh in from Buenos Aires in Argentina and São Paulo in Brazil as well as from Cochabamba and La Paz, and from the size of the awaiting crowds one might judge that half the city turns out to meet them. Once through the shabby pink terminal building, passengers emerge into a patio edged with brilliant bougainvillea bushes and dark green mango trees, affording some protection from the scorching sun that sets air waves shimmering over the flat surrounding countryside.

The city of Santa Cruz is level also, looking a bit like a Western town in a cowboy movie. Sidewalks in the center of town run high enough above street level to make it easy for riders to dismount from their steeds—and occasionally one sees a horseman from the plains doing just that. Few of the buildings are more than two stories high. On their tile roofs are little forests of cactus and succulent plants that have sprouted all by themselves, and bromeliads shaped like spiky little balls cling to light and telephone wires overhead.

During mornings and afternoons, the main square, Plaza 24 de Septiembre, and the narrow streets leading to it are crammed with people: students from the local university with its plastered-over holes made during the revolution led by Colonel Banzer, himself a cruceño; drivers waiting while their trucks are unloaded; shoppers making purchases at drugstores, markets, clothing and dry goods stores, record shops, and furniture outlets. From noon to two o'clock, however, the place seems deserted. Stores close and just about everybody is home for the *siesta,* the nap customary in towns and cities throughout many parts of Latin America for escaping the midday heat.

Restaurants are about the only commercial establishments to stay open. *Churrasquerías,* or steak houses, are favorites, and the most common order is *chuleta de res con papas*—beefsteak with fried potatoes. Another local dish is *locro,* a sort of stew or soup made of rice and dried meat called *charqui,* with potatoes, turnips, or other roots. Although fruit is plentiful in the area, better restaurants serve only the canned variety instead of the fresh bananas and papayas and mangoes which any poor person is likely to have growing in his backyard. The dark coffee in tiny cups is delicious. Some of the best-tasting coffee in the world is grown in the Oriente, in clearings beneath the shade of towering trees.

Late afternoon is a good time to visit the botanical garden on the city's outskirts. Here are huge trees, the remnants of a stand of dense tropical forest, as well as cactus gardens and grassy glades and knolls, favorite spots for picnickers on Sundays and holidays. Tiny deer called *urinas,* about the size of a poodle, graze unconcernedly in the shade. Tree specimens include *tipo, cedro, toborochi, ochoo,* and *mara,* all excellent for furniture and building timbers, especially the majestic mara with its straight trunk sixty to eighty feet high.

Along the circular avenues ringing the older part of the city, new homes of brick and concrete are going up in the modern style, with lawns and gardens. Some are the residences of merchants and farm owners for whom the Oriente's boom, with its rising land prices, has brought new prosperity. One neighborhood is dubbed "petroleum village" because its occupants

Enormous bundles of sugarcane await processing at a mill near Santa Cruz.

are mostly officials of Yacimientos Petrolíferos Fiscales Bolivianos, commonly known simply by its initials YPFB, the government oil company operating the oil fields in the Santa Cruz Department. Where one of the avenues crosses a main entry to the city stands a statue of Christ, poised on an immense steel tripod, the tallest structure in the city. Nearby is the city's only motel. The large swimming pool with its snack bar is a favorite gathering spot for young people on hot Saturday afternoons.

A paved highway runs northward toward the town of Montero and the *poblaciones,* the settlements of people from the high valleys and the altiplano as well as from other countries. One of them, now grown into a full-scale town, is made up of immigrants from the Japanese-owned island of Okinawa and is appropriately named "Okinawa." There are colonies of Italians, and some of the German Mennonite families chose this area, while others settled southwest of Santa Cruz.

For a time, the highway snakes across sandy, semiarid soil typical of Santa Cruz and its environs. A two-foot lizard, called a *veni,* scuttles across the highway. A pair of *tordos,* black thrushes that can imitate sounds like the myna birds of Southeast Asia, dart at a hawk to force it away from their nest. Big trucks come rumbling along with huge logs for the sawmills in Santa Cruz. They have come from Yapacuní, a town on the river with the same name and the present terminus of the paved highway. Like the Piray, a muddy, shifting river that skirts Santa Cruz city to the west, the Yapacuní is a tributary of the Mamoré River, which changes its name to the Madeira after it enters Brazil and joins the Amazon to flow into the Atlantic.

Near the town of Warnes, the highway enters a zone of loamier, darker earth, much better suited to agriculture. It runs past broad fields of cotton, the bursting bolls looking like snow that had fallen the night before. Large brown birds called rheas, smaller relatives of the ostrich, stalk up and down the rows looking for insects to eat. There are lush fields of rice, tobacco, corn, and sugar. Agriculture here is a far cry from the simple methods of cultivating small plots with primitive tools so typical of the altiplano. Fields here are extensive, allowing tractors and other farm machines to be used. And once in a while, one can see a low-flying crop-dusting plane zooming up at the end of its run. All about is evidence that Santa Cruz is well on its way to the next stage of development: industries to process its agricultural and mineral products. There are already sugar mills, plants to gin cotton and crush oil from the seeds, rice-drying beds, and sawmills. Scheduled to come soon is a factory to make fertilizers from the region's natural gas.

After Warnes, the next town is Montero, a miniature Santa Cruz and a reminder of how that city looked only a few years back. There are the same low buildings with colonnades supporting roofs over the sidewalks, but the streets are generally filled with mud or choking dust. The town has a frontier atmosphere, with barbershops open to the street, numerous bars, and an occasional family pig taking its ease in the dust. But more motorcycles than horses are seen. In fact, motorcycles are used as taxis in many parts of the Oriente, and in the Montero area it is far from unusual to see one racing along with an Aymara woman sitting sideways behind the driver, holding her derby hat in place with one hand while her ropelike braid of black hair swings with the breeze. Another transportation curiosity in the region is the autos equipped with flanged steel wheels that serve as buses on the Santa Cruz–Corumbá railway.

In the area around Montero and Warnes, some of the Indians from the highlands work their own lands, but many hire themselves out as day laborers to work on large plantations. Trucks pick them up at gathering spots early in the morning and return them in the evening. Their homes are no longer the stone and adobe huts of the altiplano, but are made of bamboo poles and have steeply pitched roofs thatched with palm leaves.

The pioneers from the altiplano have had little difficulty in adjusting to the climate of the Oriente lowlands, contrary to predictions. Yet, paradoxically, it has been harder for them to become assimilated into Santa Cruz society than for the immigrants from foreign lands. There is a hostility between the Indians and their fellow Bolivians of Santa Cruz. The light-skinned cruceños, with little or no Indian blood, resent the newly arrived highlanders and talk about them in "we-they" terms, or *nosotros y ellos* in Spanish. "They wouldn't give you a glass of water if you were dying of thirst," says a cruceño bitterly. For their part, the Quechuas and Aymaras, for generations exploited by descendants of the Spanish conquistadores, are timid and quite naturally tend to keep to themselves. But they are still coming to both Santa Cruz and the Beni Department, wherever roads are opened. Altogether, the government's National Colonization Institute says that more than two hundred thousand people from the highlands have been settled on 2.5 million acres of territory in the Oriente.

While pushing colonization and agriculture in this region, Bolivia is also at work developing the area's subsoil wealth, of which oil and natural gas are the most promising components. Today eastern Bolivia's petroleum output is only around sixty thousand barrels a day—a mere trickle when compared with 3.5 million for Venezuela—but the jungle areas on the eastern flanks of the Andes and the adjoining flatlands as far north as Ecuador have yielded important discoveries in recent years, and the Bolivians are intensifying their search. Nor are they overlooking the altiplano. At Vilque, near the salt flats of Uyuni, test wells have been sunk to depths of ten thousand feet.

The newest fields in production, however, are north of Santa Cruz around Naranjillos and at Bulo-Bulo, where a tiny airstrip has been hacked out of the jungle. Getting heavy equipment such as drilling rigs and big diesel engines into areas such as these where there are no roads is a tiring and hazardous job. Machinery has to be dragged across rough terrain, rafted across rivers, or hauled dangling from cables stretched from bank to bank.

The oldest fields in the Camiri region southeast of Santa Cruz are still the most important, however. Camiri is near the region where Che Guevara tried to organize a guerrilla movement to overthrow the government, and it is easy to see how his band was able to elude capture for so long. It is irregular country, full of ravines and cliffs and *elevadores* or "elevators," the local term for rocky, mountainous terrain. Guevara was able to operate for months in this harsh wilderness, before his capture by Bolivian Army rangers in a final ambush at a place called Quebrada del Yuro.

Camiri is still the main center of YPFB's petroleum production activities, and it boasts a refinery besides. From Camiri, oil is pumped to the high valleys and the altiplano, and to the Chilean port of Arica. Another pipeline takes oil to Argentina, and in 1972, a 332-mile pipeline to carry gas from Colpa in Santa Cruz to Argentina was inaugurated. Now the Bolivians have agreed to sell gas to Brazil also, via a pipeline to be built all the way to São Paulo. As part of the deal, Brazil is to help

Bolivia build a steel mill to make steel from the iron ore deposits around Mutún, in the southeast corner of Santa Cruz Department near the Brazilian border. Ore from these deposits is already being sold to Argentina.

In fact, Bolivia seems to be reaping many rewards from the rivalry between its two biggest neighbors—although some Bolivians think the battle for economic influence in Bolivia is a threat to their country's security and territorial integrity. Both Brazil and Argentina are helping Bolivia extend its inadequate highway (17,250 miles, of which only 1,000 are paved) and railway networks. The Brazilians have offered to finance a

An Indian house in the tropical lowlands.

highway paralleling the Corumbá–Santa Cruz rail line and are ready to join forces with Bolivia in constructing the missing Santa Cruz–Cochabamba rail link. For their part, the Argentines are extending the railroad they built to Santa Cruz all the way north to Yapacuní, on the edge of Bolivia's last frontier, the Beni and Pando departments.

# 10

---

# The Beni and the Pando—Bolivia's Last Frontier

No sooner did the sixteenth-century European explorers begin probing their way along the coasts of Central and South America when they heard stories from native peoples of a kingdom so rich its ruler powdered his body with gold dust. The discoverers searched far and wide for the abode of El Dorado, the Gilded Man, but it was always just over the next mountain range, deep within some forest, or somewhere far upstream on one of the mysterious rivers. The Pizarro brothers listened avidly to such tales. So did the English explorer Sir Walter Raleigh, who believed that the way to Eldorado—for the name came to signify the place as well as its king—lay up the Orinoco River.

Actually these legends were exaggerated accounts of the Inca empire, unrecognized as their ultimate goal by the Spaniards who conquered Cuzco. Instead, they were convinced that even greater wealth awaited them in the jungles east of the Andean ramparts, possibly in a realm called Paititi, of which the Jaguar Lord, Musu, or Mojo, was the monarch. In the course of a century, many expeditions—from the Andes as well as from Spanish settlements in the *pampas,* or plains, of Argentina and Paraguay—set out to conquer El Gran Mojo. Their journeys took them to what is today Bolivia's Beni Department, the eastern part of which appears on maps as the Mojos Plains. No mighty civilization was ever discovered there, nor any city of gold, but only leagues and leagues of dense tropical forest and grasslands, thinly peopled with tribes of fierce Indians the Spanish soldiers could not dominate.

Even with all his marvelous technology, modern man is far from having conquered the Beni, which together with the neighboring Pando Department is Bolivia's last frontier. These two departments together account for more than half of Bolivia's Oriente, the East, although the Pando is actually a thin strip facing northwest and bordering the Brazilian state of Acre. They make up Bolivia's share of the vast Amazon basin, which also takes in half of Brazil and parts of Peru, Ecuador, Colombia, and Venezuela. The eastern part of the Beni is a tossing ocean of windblown grass, practically unbroken by roads and with thickets of trees in places near the rivers. But most of the Beni and virtually all of the Pando is jungle, and is more remote from the rest of Bolivia than even Santa Cruz.

Before the era of aviation, it was easier to reach the Beni and the Pando by boat from Europe and the United States than overland from La Paz. Even today there is nothing anywhere in the region that deserves to be called a highway. The "roads" are the twisting rivers, full of rapids and sluggish stretches hiding dangerous snags. Although maps are sprinkled with dots representing towns, most of them are nothing more than a street leading back from a river between two rows of houses with peeling plaster, or a collection of thatched huts mounted on stilts to protect them from floods.

Penetrating this wild region was difficult enough for the soldiers of Spain, but bringing it under their influence and establishing any kind of permanent outposts proved too much for them, as it had for the troops of the Incas. However, a different sort of invaders—peaceful ones—had more success, although they too had to pay a price. They were the Jesuit missionaries who had followed Ñuflo de Chavez to Santa Cruz. Taking their cue from the Chiriguani Indians of Santa Cruz, who were trading iron tools and other Spanish products with the peoples of the Mojos, the Jesuit fathers also decided to become merchants and follow up with efforts to make converts to Christianity. Although several were expelled and others lost their lives, the Jesuits had managed to establish permanent missions in the Beni by the late 1600s.

What they found there were people who were planters and skilled craftsmen, living in small villages connected by earthen causeways that remained above water in flood seasons. They raised crops—yucca, peanuts, sweet potatoes, bananas, cotton, corn, and sugarcane—and made rush baskets and beautiful capes or robes of feathers. Gradually the Jesuits taught them other crafts and arts. They brought cattle to the region, which soon multiplied into vast herds, then horses, and taught the *mojeños*, the people of the Mojos, how to ride so that they could become cowboys.

But the Jesuits' work all came to an end in 1767, when they were expelled from all of South America, on the orders of the Pope in Rome, at the behest of colonists who resented the Jesuits' influence over the Indians and the prosperous landholdings under the Jesuits' control. Their missions were pillaged and soon fell into ruins. The Indians were driven away or drafted as forced labor. Churches which once had echoed with the singing of Indian choirs were stripped of their silver and gold, part of which the Bolivians used to help finance their war for independence.

For years afterward, governments gave thought to the Beni only for what they could take out of it with the least effort. To pay for services rendered, they often issued letters entitling the holder to so many head of cattle—but it was up to him to collect them, and nobody was around to keep a strict count. The half-wild cattle were rounded up, some to be slaughtered on the spot merely for the hides and others to be sent on long drives to markets in Argentina. Soon the herds of Mojos cattle that had grown into millions were decimated. The Indians too—those who survived the breakup of the missions—died by the thousands of white men's diseases like measles and influenza, against which they had no natural immunity.

As for the jungle region to the west and north, a demand for two natural products brought sudden wealth in the late nineteenth and early twentieth centuries to a few entrepreneurs tough enough to withstand its rigors. One of the products was quinine, a substance extracted from the bark of the cinchona tree helpful in combating malaria and other fevers. The other was rubber. Both were collected by Indians working for traders like the *hermanos* Suaréz, the Suaréz brothers, who ruled their empire from headquarters at Cachuela Esperanza, Waterfalls of Hope, on the Beni River. Sent by river craft downstream to Amazon ports and thence by steamships to Europe and the United States, the rubber and cinchona brought fat profits to the traders. They paid the Indians in food and liquor, knives and cloth and other manufactures, always managing to keep the gatherers in debt so they had no other choice but to keep on working. The traders lived like veritable kings, importing pianos and phonographs and other luxuries from abroad, since there was little to spend their money on in the Amazon region. To help them increase their profits by reducing transportation costs, the Brazilian government, in exchange for an agreement by Bolivia to cede some of its territory, built a railway around some impassable rapids on the Madeira River. The railroad was completed just when cheaper rubber from plantations in Southeast Asia spelled the collapse of the boom for Amazonian rubber, which had to be collected from trees growing widely separated in the jungle. As for cinchona, cheaper synthetic products just about ended the market for quinine.

Some natural rubber, however, still comes out of the Beni, produced in the traditional way. Gatherers, called *siringeros,* after the name for the rubber tree, *siringuera,* make the rounds of 150 to 200 trees daily to collect the white sticky latex that oozes from slanting gashes cut in the bark and drips into tiny cups. At curing stations, a sort of paddle is alternately dipped into pans of latex and turned over a smoky fire until the liquid becomes a gum. When the resulting ball of gum is a couple of feet in diameter, it is removed from the paddle or stick and is ready for shipment to factories.

Once again, as in Santa Cruz, transportation is the key to future development of the Beni and Pando. To be sure, a few makeshift roads that are little more than oxcart or Jeep trails link some of the towns within the region, but what is needed are all-weather highways to the outside. Governments have made plans to build a road to connect with the Cochabamba–Santa Cruz paved highway, to extend the yungas' roads farther into the jungles, and to extend the road leading north from Santa Cruz all the way to the Beni. But work has hardly begun, and the costs of construction are staggering. Meanwhile, people and goods move into and out of the two depart-

The airfield at Magdalena, where a cargo plane is due from the town of Trinidad, 150 miles away.

ments by water and air—by rivers flowing into Brazil and by plane to the altiplano. Dozens of landing strips suitable for small planes and the veteran DC-3's of the Bolivian Air Force have been hacked out of jungle growth. Products such as rubber, coffee, cocoa—and even timber—are flown to the highlands despite the astronomic cost, because that is the only practical way of getting them there. Many of the larger *estancias,* or ranches, in the Mojos Plains have landing strips and planes of their own.

No one can do much traveling in the Beni-Pando region, however, without making use of its rivers. There are hundreds. Some, like the Mamoré, the Madre de Dios (Mother of God), the Iténez (called the Guaporé in Brazil), the Orión, the Tahuamanu, and the Beni itself are immense, yet they are practically unknown to the world outside Bolivia. They writhe like snakes across grasslands or through the *selva,* the tropical forest, virtually unchanged from its primitive state except for an occasional clearing with the thatched hut, or *barraca,* of a rubber gatherer and his family. Even the biggest rivers are difficult to navigate, for they are interrupted by rapids or filled with obstacles such as sunken trees and treacherous shifting sandbars.

A variety of craft are used on the rivers, ranging from a type of canoe hollowed out from a single log and often powered by an outboard motor to small diesel-engine cargo and passenger vessels. There are rafts, called balsas like the totora-reed craft of the Lake Titicaca fishermen but made from light balsa-wood logs, and the larger *callapos,* consisting of three parts joined by wooden crosspieces. Cumbersome *batelones,* heavy wooden rowboats manned by a dozen or more oarsmen and carrying a thatched housing at the rear, are still found, although they are much less common than at the height of the rubber trade.

A balsa trip on one of Bolivia's swift rivers can be a harrowing experience. Passengers sit on a platform of split bamboo raised slightly above the logs, which are fastened together with wooden pegs. The *balseros,* or raftsmen, stand at either end armed with long poles to fend against threatening rocks. For a while, the balsa drifts smoothly through quiet pools. A *jacaré*, or alligator, snoozing on a sandbank, raises his head and then splashes into the water. The splash sends a band of green parrots screeching off over the trees.

Now the raft picks up speed as the current rushes toward a stretch of rapids. Soon the tiny craft is moving with frightening swiftness, bobbing its way past tall cliffs, between rocks, through chutes where waves crash together to hurl fountains of water into the air. The raftsmen are busy every second, their eyes peeled for hidden rocks, thrusting their poles against steep banks, fighting to keep the balsa from turning sideways. Finally the raft glides into another peaceful stretch, and the balseros sink to their knees in exhaustion.

The selva, too, is fraught with hazards and filled with strange creatures, both real and imaginary. The huge trees with showy orchids and bromeliads clinging to their trunks and branches tower above the undergrowth of ferns, prickly vines, and creepers. Along stream banks, bushes grow so densely they have to be slashed away to make a passage. The multiplicity of plant life is overwhelming. There are over two thousand species of trees alone, all mixed together without the large stands of one variety often found in the Northern Hemisphere.

South America does not have very large animals such as are found in Africa and other parts of the world, except perhaps for the boa constrictor or anaconda, a snake that reaches twenty feet or more in length. What the animal population lacks in size, it makes up in variety. Besides the small deer called urinas, the otters, the monkeys, the spotted jaguars and other cats, the jungle animals include the tapir, which has a flexible trunk about a foot long; the anteater, with a curved snout so narrow it looks like a beak, a thin tongue to probe down antholes, and a plumelike tail; the *tatú*, or armadillo, covered by a shell and with sharp claws for tunneling into the earth; and the sloth, which crawls along tree branches hanging upside down from its scythelike claws. Besides the large boa constrictors, snakes include the deadly bushmaster and several types so long and thin they can easily be mistaken for the vines to which they cling. There are brilliant birds; most are small and live high in the treetops, so they are difficult to spot, but they also include the giant macaws with their plumage of blue and yellow, or red and blue, as well as the comical looking *tucanos,* or toucans. The huge yellow beaks of the toucans are powerful enough to crack nuts, but they can delicately pluck a berry or small fruit from a branch without crushing it. The bird then tilts back its head and lets the fruit roll down into its throat.

Rivers in the Beni and Pando teem with fish, including the eighty- to one-hundred-pound "general," the *pacú,* and the *surubí,* all of which are delicious to eat. There are also the dreaded *pirañas.* The taste or odor of fresh blood attracts pirañas in swarms, and it is no myth that they can shred the flesh of a living being—man or animal—in a matter of minutes. But the reported behavior of another creature is almost certainly untrue—or at least has never been verified. This is a sort of kingfisher that supposedly rubs a certain plant against cliffs to soften up the rock so it can peck out holes for its nest.

Insects are the most troublesome creatures encountered in the Beni-Pando region. There are tiny ticks, almost invisible to the naked eye, and dozens of flies and mosquitoes. Some are always getting into people's eyes; others go for the ankles; one type called the *borro* lays its eggs under the skin of men and animals, and when the larvae hatch they form painful abscesses which have to be cut out.

Anyone who enters the selva expecting the air to be constantly filled with the chattering of *monos,* monkeys, and the weird cries of birds is due for a disappointment. The tropical forest's most overwhelming characteristic is its stillness. The strange squawks and chattering are there, but they come at infrequent intervals. The noisiest creatures are the frogs and tree toads, croaking and thumping at night. Another surprise is that, while the climate is normally hot, the Beni can also be chilly. In the winter months of June through August, cold winds called *surazos* often blow from the south, bringing sudden drops in the temperature.

With all its difficulties and lurking hazards, the selva is far from being inhospitable to man. The forest Indians—remnants of once numerous tribes—are perfectly at home, adapting their lives to the environment rather than trying to change it, living in much the same simple way as uncounted generations of their ancestors, who carried on trade with the highland peoples before and during the reign of the Incas. Raising food in the fertile, well-watered soil of the jungle does not require the same kind of painstaking labor as on the altiplano. On forest clearings, the Indians raise yucca, corn, squash, and beans, which they supplement with fish from the rivers and wild game, including armadillos and monkeys. When the soil loses its strength, the Indians simply bundle up their few belongings—their baskets, hammocks, and clay cooking vessels, their bows and arrows and other implements—and move to a new area where they make fresh clearings.

Slowly—very slowly—the jungle is giving ground to the bulldozers of highway construction teams, the saws of lumbermen,

A woman of the Chacobo tribe in the Beni flattens tree bark to make a kind of cloth called *tipoy*.

and the axes and machetes of settlers. In some places, machines have cleared land for settlements under the government's program of encouraging people to shift from the highlands to the Oriente. But for the most part such people make their own *chaqueos,* or clearings, where corn and yucca sprout among charred tree stumps. Their simple huts, or *pawiches,* made of bark and palm thatch are grouped along trails or at river landings. Add a trading post and a store or two, and this is the way a village starts. Villages grow into towns, important enough for the government to establish an army post or a civil administrative center. Perhaps a diesel generator is brought in, and the town has electric lights, which flicker and go out for the night around nine o'clock. With a school or a hospital, the town is now on its way to becoming a small city.

So far, only a handful of places in the whole vast region have attained that status. Trinidad, the largest city and the capital of the Beni Department, has a population of twenty-three thousand. As in the small towns of Santa Cruz, motorcycles here serve as taxis. Riberalta, located strategically at the juncture of the Madre de Dios and the Beni rivers, is only half that size. The center of Bolivia's rubber and Brazil nut gathering industries, Riberalta has streets "paved" with grass, testifying to the scantiness of traffic. Cobija, the sleepy capital of the Pando almost at the northwest corner of Bolivia, has only five thousand inhabitants. Other towns such as Reyes, Rurrenabaque, San Borja, and Porvenir are important enough centers to appear on maps, but in reality they are little more than isolated cattle towns or river-front collection points, often under flood waters, for the rubber and Brazil nut trade.

For sportsmen and adventurous persons who simply want to experience life in an exotic, out-of-the-way corner of the world, there are small hotels that usually charge by the bed. Since there are generally four or more beds to a room, anyone wanting a room to himself must pay for all the beds. In addition, a place to stay can often be found at a missionary center or on one of the estancias.

Life in the Beni and the Pando revolves around work and the pleasures of outdoor life, for there is little organized entertainment. Movie houses, for example, are few and far between. Where they exist, they are extremely popular, for there is no television anywhere in the area. The arrival of a plane or a government mission from La Paz is a big event. Important visitors have to go through a long schedule of lunches and speeches and dinners. Fiestas, or holidays, come at different times from those elsewhere in Bolivia, and the big one held on November 18 is called the Fiesta of the Beni. There are bands, athletic events, dancing groups carrying wooden swords giving imitations of Spanish bullfights, and the old custom of contestants trying to climb to the top of a greased pole where some prize has been fastened.

While access to the Beni and the Pando remains so difficult, life in the region will continue its leisurely, unsophisticated pace. The roads are coming, a mile or two at a time. However, one activity could hasten their arrival. Bolivia's Amazon basin area is part of the huge lowland crescent east of the Andes which geologists believe may contain enormous petroleum deposits. In fact, oil is already flowing out of the eastern jungles of Colombia, Ecuador, and Peru. With the world hungry for fuel, an intensive hunt for more by oil men from half a dozen countries is now under way through the region, including Bolivia's frontier Department of the Beni.

# 11

---

# The People and Their Customs

In all of Bolivia there are only five million people, hardly enough to make a single large city as population standards go these days. Yet, generalizing about them, attempting to draw a composite picture of the Bolivian, is harder than trying to describe a "typical" resident of the United States, a country with forty times more inhabitants than Bolivia has. In fact, it is an impossible task, for besides being distributed over an area the size of France and Spain combined, with striking contrasts in geography and climate, the Bolivians are sharply divided in ethnic and language backgrounds, as well as modes of living. In many if not most ways, the Aymara fisherman of Lake Titicaca is as different from the doctor or lawyer of nearby La Paz, who may have studied in Europe or the United States, as the Eskimo is from a citizen of almost any small town or large metropolis in the industrial society of North America.

More than half of Bolivia's people—an estimated 55 percent—are Indians, primarily the Aymaras and Quechuas of the altiplano and the high valleys, but including remnants of the primitive Uros and Chipayas and the lowland tribes as well. Living for the most part in their own communities and following their own pattern of life, the Indians form virtually a separate society. Only about 15 percent of the Bolivians are of pure or almost pure European descent, mostly Spanish but with a smattering of German, Italian, and other nationalities represented also. Socially, if not always economically, these people are at the top of the ladder. Except for a sprinkling of peoples such as Lebanese and the Japanese settlers in Santa Cruz, the remaining 30 percent are cholos, a mixture of Indian and European, with an occasional drop of African blood inherited from the few black slaves imported as servants by the wealthy miners of Potosí. The cholos constitute the bulk of Bolivia's urban workers and small middle class.

Although his physical characteristics are markedly Indian, the stocky cholo tends to identify himself with the European in outlook and life-style. He follows the European or Western fashion in clothing, for example, and speaks Spanish as his first language, although many can also understand Aymara or Quechua. He can be as indifferent or disdainful toward those peoples, many of whom speak only their own tongues, as the haughtiest Bolivian of pure Spanish origin. Yet paradoxically the cholo is generally proud of his own Indian heritage, which he often traces back to some Inca princess, although in all likelihood it came to him through a kitchen servant one of his Spanish forebears took a fancy to. The cholo is energetic, restless, ambitious. Of the three main types of people he is the most self-confident of his role as a Bolivian—more so than most Spanish-descended Bolivians, who are sensitive about being citizens of a poor country and, as in aristocratic Sucre, often tend to dwell in the past; infinitely more so than the Indians, whose concern seldom passes the limits of their own villages and whose loyalties above all are to their ancient traditions and folkways, in part because they have been made to feel outcasts in their own country.

Even among the Indians, moreover, there is division. The Aymaras and the Quechuas, the two main groups, keep their separate distinctions and seldom intermarry. Both peoples were ruled by the Incas, who made Quechua the official language of the realm but allowed the Aymaras to retain their own tongue also. Aloof, shy in the presence of strangers—the stolid Aymaras more so than the cheerful Quechuas—the Indians keep themselves pretty much spiritually apart from their fellow Bolivians, remaining faithful to their ancestral beliefs and mountain gods, who often appear disguised as Christian saints.

Highly dependent on the powerful forces of nature, the Indians believe nearly all natural objects have souls. Each mountain peak is the home of an *achichila,* or spirit, with a special interest in the people of the nearest village. When an Aymara crosses a ridge to another valley and first sees a summit, he doffs his hat, kneels, and makes an offering to the achichila of the wad of coca leaves he happens to be chewing. The earth goddess, Pacha Mama, protective of men and animals if they respect her, angry and vengeful if they do not, ranks first in the Indian's pantheon, and the old custom of *ch'allar,* spilling a few drops of a drink on the ground to honor her, persists.

Many animals have special significance for the Indians. Thus it is a good omen when one sees a condor or a jaguar, or especially a vicuña, but a bad sign to come across an armadillo. To see a moth means someone close is about to die. A lizard held next to the skin can cure illnesses. Indians as well as most cholos are firm believers in ghosts, and to learn what is going to happen they consult a *yatiri,* or fortune-teller, who predicts the future by watching the way coca leaves fall when tossed on a piece of cloth or by examining the wad someone has been chewing.

The Indians have a story or myth to account for the origin of nearly everything. Rain, for example, is the work of Huiratata, the father-wind and husband of Pacha Mama, who draws water from the rivers and lakes and then pours it back over the earth. The national flower kantuta sprang from drops of blood shed by an Indian princess who fell into a ravine and died while on her way to visit her lover, a handsome young man, but of lowly birth, whom she was not allowed to marry.

More than half of Bolivia's people take such beliefs to heart. Yet at the same time, other Bolivians are flying jet airplanes, maintaining microwave communications equipment in working order, performing surgery, and operating oil-drilling rigs. And by no means do the paths of people with such radically different backgrounds never cross. On the contrary, they rub shoulders everyday, often providing some startling contrasts, at least in the eyes of visitors.

An Eskimo clad in his sealskins on a street corner in the capital of the United States certainly would draw stares. But in downtown La Paz, no one casts a second glance at a young Indian mother, her feet in slipperlike shoes of soft llama leather and her baby riding on her back, as she thumbs through a home and garden magazine in front of a newsstand. She may not understand a word of the Spanish text—about 60 percent of Bolivians can neither read nor write in any language—but she is fascinated by the pictures. One in particular holds her attention; it shows the living room of a well-to-do Bolivian family, and on a shelf sits a comical ceramic figure weighted down with packages. It is a representation of the ancient Inca divinity Ekeko, who brings good fortune and presents to his devotees. Nearly every home in Bolivia has one of these little *alacitas,* or miniatures, including that of the young Indian woman herself. The rest of the objects in the photo—the beautiful furniture and the gleaming appliances—she could never hope to own. Nevertheless, she does have a sewing machine, and the shawl her baby is wrapped in is factory-made.

Such a scene reveals much about ways of living in Bolivia. It has no single culture, but rather a rich and varied pattern produced by people of diverse backgrounds who go pretty much in their own directions but are ready to borrow from one another when it seems feasible and useful to do so.

The process of interchange dates from the earliest colonial times when the Spaniards, who rarely brought their own wives to the New World with them, took to marrying Indian women, thereby giving rise to the cholos, or the Race of Bronze, as one Bolivian author put it. The Spaniards quickly adopted such local food as corn and cocoa and the little peppers from which the *aji* sauce, a hot seasoning used throughout the altiplano, is made. The Spanish priests set about converting the Indians to Catholicism. For the most part, they succeeded only in superimposing Christianity on the pagan beliefs of the Indians, who readily identified some of the saints and biblical characters with their own deities. Possibly because they felt the more gods there were the better, many simply accepted the new religion while continuing to render homage to the old.

In a later period, native-born craftsmen grafted local plant and animal forms in stone to the churches they helped to build, in what became known as the mestizo, or mixed, style of architecture. And the Indians and cholos incorporated Spanish music and dancing, especially the latter, into their own art forms. The popular *cueca,* for example, with its bows and rapid stamping called the *zapateo* at the end of each section or movement, stems directly from the stately courtship *flamenco*

Aymara men wearing traditional *llucho* caps take part in Catholic holiday in La Paz.

dances of old Spain. The borrowing process is still going on. More modern styles of clothing are being adopted by the altiplano Indians, even the standoffish Aymaras, whose menfolk are starting to wear the traditional garb of the cholos, a soft felt hat and a black suit, with a scarf tucked under the coat in winter.

Despite their many differences, Bolivians of all walks of life, regardless of background, do seem to have a number of traits in common. They tend to be much more formal in social relations than North Americans, for example. This does not mean they are any less friendly, but merely reflects the weight they give to politeness and good manners. No one likes to say "no," because it might offend. Some softer, indirect way of giving a negative response, one that generally includes an excuse, is used. People shake hands whenever they meet, even though they have known one another for years. Men who are close friends usually follow up the handshake by patting each other on the back with their right hands. When entering a room, it is customary to greet those already present, although they may be total strangers. The formality and careful courtesy increase the farther one gets away from the cities into the sparsely populated countryside. When some passenger on a lonely stretch of road boards a bus, he tips his hat, and a litany of *"Buenos dias"* or *"Buenas tardes"*—"Good morning," "Good afternoon"—follows him all the way as he moves down the aisle to find a seat. Bolivians make light of difficulties. *"No hay problema"*—"There's no problem"—they will say, even when there decidedly is one. But this is their way, for example, of reassuring a traveler whose car has broken down, and of showing willingness to help, even in situations when there is really little anyone can do to be helpful.

The insistence on personal dignity—the quality of masculine pride and honor called *machismo* in Spanish—is also highly valued. It must be respected, for insults are never taken lightly, and a knife or revolver may be drawn to wipe one out. A Bolivian will go to great lengths to have the last word, for being bested in an argument means losing face. Sometimes when arguments run out of logic, they degenerate into a sort of battle of *dichos,* short, pithy sayings or proverbs that sum up a point of view or state a truism, and Bolivians seem to have one to fit any set of circumstances. "Anybody who works doesn't have time to make money" may be the reply of someone admonished about his gambling. "One hand washes the other" is another way of saying "You help me and I'll help you." And "A cat that meows is a poor hunter" is a phrase designed to silence someone who has been boasting.

Bolivians pay a great deal of attention to personal appearance and careful grooming. No town, no matter how small, is without a peluquería, barber shop, or two, often kept wide open so customers can see what is going on in the street while they have their hair cut. The men ask the barbers to use plenty of brilliantine, and they like being doused with the sweet-smelling liquids from the colored bottles. All classes of people have a liking for fine-looking clothing, since the way one dresses is a symbol of his wealth or social standing in the community. Upper-class men wear finely tailored suits of imported tropical worsted or tweeds, depending on the season. Their wives like to take flying shopping trips to Buenos Aires, or São Paulo or Lima, where the latest fashions arrive sooner than in La Paz. No one can understand the North American's deliberately casual dress and fondness for old clothes, not even the young people. Although they have picked up the blue-jeans-and-denim-shirt outfit popular in the United States, those garments always look freshly laundered and ironed. The wardrobes of boys and girls of well-off families include beautiful alpaca-wool sweaters and ponchos with Indian designs, but only since they attained a certain chic abroad.

The Indians have gaudy clothing to be brought out on feast days, in striking contrast with the drabness of their everyday wear. For men, the holiday best consists of a short, tight-fitting jacket and bell-bottom trousers, lavishly decorated with sequins and embroidery. Women wear handsomely embroidered blouses and flamboyant skirts over a multitude of petticoats—sometimes twenty or more—of different hues. As for their hats, they are usually the Indian woman's proudest possessions. No matter how poor she may be, she always has several kept spic and span for days when she dresses up.

Family and kinship play highly important roles in the lives of Bolivians, more so than among North Americans. In the first place, Bolivian families are generally larger, both in terms of the number of children a couple may have and in the extent of familial relationships. When he speaks of his "family," the Bolivian as likely as not is thinking of all its members, from grandparents and great-aunts and uncles to first and second cousins—in short, everybody with a blood or marital tie that makes him or her a member of a "clan." All within it count on one another for support and help in everything from voting to providing jobs. Furthermore, the concept of family is even broader, extending to the artificial relationship of godparents, who play important and lasting roles in the life of every Bolivian. Godparents are chosen carefully, for much more is expected of them than simply showing up for the christening. If anything should happen to the real parents, the godparents become responsible for the upbringing of the child. Within families, the *padriño* and *madriña*, godfather and godmother, are generally persons of equal social status, but wealthy persons are often asked to be godparents of a child in some humble family as a means of assuring him prominent and powerful patrons who can help him throughout life. The bond between a child's parents and his godparents is recognized and enduring: They are *compadres* and *comadres*, co-fathers and co-mothers.

Bolivians love to talk. They enjoy gossiping about neighbors, and any departure from normal standards of conduct sets tongues wagging, often inventively. Thus whatever *fulano*, so-and-so, may have said or done is the subject of lively comment at gatherings of friends and at family reunions. A close rival as a topic of conversation is politics, which is a deadly serious business in Bolivia, as the country's frequent government overthrows and revolutions attest. Political leaders flit back and forth across the borders with regularity, biding their time while abroad until another change in government makes it safe for them to return. The custom of granting amnesty is part of the rules of the game, however, and many an exile's plight has been eased by a government announcement around Christmas of a list of political offenders whose misdeeds have been forgiven.

While politics is a powerful element among the forces dividing Bolivian society, music and sports are unifying influences. Whether produced by traditional native instruments—wooden flutes, strings, and all sorts of drums and other noisemakers— or the brass horns of the industrial age, the sound of a band always attracts a crowd. Taking the family to the concert by the band of the fire department or the militia or the police academy is a regular Sunday afternoon chore for fathers in most cities and large towns. The growing number of Indians who own transistor radios listen with enthusiasm to whatever popular music is being played, whether it be the dance rhythms of the cueca or the *bailecito,* both reminiscent of Spain, or their own *huayño,* dating from Inca days.

Nearly every type of sport is played one place or another in Bolivia. The Japanese settlements in the Oriente even organize baseball teams to play among themselves, but the game is unknown elsewhere. Tennis, basketball, volleyball, swimming, boxing, and wrestling are popular, but one game has absolute ascendance over all others. It is soccer, or *fútbol,* as it is called throughout Latin America. It is the one game in Bolivia that just about everybody understands and every boy has played.

Campesinos playing the traditional *zampona* pipes.

From the altiplano to the lowlands, a level space with goal posts at either end is one of the easiest things to spot from the air when a plane is approaching an airport or rough landing strip. Boys start playing the game almost as soon as they can walk, and stars on the most important professional teams are national heroes, regardless of their racial origins. Bolivia once won the South America soccer championship in games played in La Paz, and the entire city went on a spree. Motorists made a din by honking their horns, people threw paper streamers and torn-up newspapers out of windows, groups marched and cheered in the streets under fluttering banners in the national colors of red, yellow, and green. The fact that the opposing teams came from cities at sea level, or at least much lower than La Paz, and were not used to strenuous action at an altitude of over twelve thousand feet made the victory no less sweet!

Because athletic events are not an integral part of academic life, young people of school age who want to participate in organized sports almost invariably must join a club. The many clubs hold social and amateur athletic events for their members, whose dues support the organizations, but they also own professional soccer teams. Rivalry among clubs, all of which have their fans among non-members, can be as intense as that between college and university teams in the United States.

Bolivian schools, on the other hand, are strictly for studying. Children start school at the age of six. Eight years of primary education is compulsory by law, but there are not enough free public schools to accommodate all who wish to attend. The government in 1973 reorganized the education system to emphasize more training in technical skills at the secondary level. Most secondary, or high, schools are privately operated, and focus their efforts on preparing students for universities and later careers in law or other professions. Today, all high schools must offer a choice of three courses. There is a *común*, or general course, and a humanities or college preparatory course, both of which offer bachelor diplomas. The third course is intended to equip young people with technical and professional skills that are in short supply in Bolivia, such as electrical maintenance and bookkeeping, so that they can get jobs immediately after graduation. Students who complete this course receive a certificate of *técnico medio*, semiskilled technician, as well as a bachelor diploma. All three high school courses are for four years. The federal government sets standards for the entire education system and operates the universities, which are free. For the Indians, there is a separate system of primary schools with instruction in their own languages.

Education—along with improved transportation—is a key factor in the future development of Bolivia as it makes headway in catching up with the twentieth century. What the Bo-

Literacy class for Indian adults near La Paz.

livians have been able to do so far, however, is no mean ac-
complishment. In fact, holding together for a century and a
half a country so divided geographically and ethnically, in the
face of a challenging and often hostile nature, without easy wa-
terways to provide a ready-made communications network as
in Europe or the United States, is in itself a remarkable
achievement and a tribute to a tenacious and proud people.

# Index

# About the Author

Leslie F. Warren has traveled widely in South America and has worked there as a journalist for more than a decade. Formerly Bureau Chief in Rio de Janeiro for *McGraw-Hill World News,* he is presently an associate editor for *Business Latin America* in Rio. Mr. Warren prepared the revision of another volume in the Portraits of the Nations series, THE LAND AND PEOPLE OF BRAZIL.